THRESHOLD
BIBLE STUDY

D1482514

JESUS,
the COMPASSIONATE
SAVIOR

PART TWO

Luke
[12–24]

STEPHEN J. BINZ

TWENTY-THIRD
PUBLICATIONS
twentythirdpublications.com

THIRD PRINTING 2019

TWENTY-THIRD PUBLICATIONS
One Montauk Avenue, Suite 200
New London, CT 06320
(860) 437-3012 or (800) 321-0411
www.twentythirdpublications.com

ISBN: 978-1-58595-873-3
Library of Congress Control Number: 2012953105
Printed in the U.S.A.

 A division of Bayard, Inc.

Contents

How to Use
Threshold Bible Study

Threshold Bible Study is a dynamic, informative, inspiring, and life-changing series that helps you learn about Scripture in a whole new way. Each book will help you explore new dimensions of faith and discover deeper insights for your life as a disciple of Jesus.

The threshold is a place of transition. The threshold of God's word invites you to enter that place where God's truth, goodness, and beauty can shine into your life and fill your mind and heart. Through the Holy Spirit, the threshold becomes holy ground, sacred space, and graced time. God can teach you best at the threshold, because God opens your life to his word and fills you with the Spirit of truth.

With *Threshold Bible Study* each topic or book of the Bible is approached in a thematic way. You will understand and reflect on the biblical texts through overarching themes derived from biblical theology. Through this method, the study of Scripture will impact your life in a unique way and transform you from within.

These books are designed for maximum flexibility. Each study is presented in a workbook format, with sections for reading, reflecting, writing, discussing, and praying. Each *Threshold* book contains thirty lessons, which you can use for your daily study over the course of a month or which can be divided into six lessons per week, providing a group study of six weekly sessions (the first session deals with the Introduction). These studies are ideal for Bible study groups, small Christian communities, adult faith formation, student groups, Sunday school, neighborhood groups, and family reading, as well as for individual learning.

The commentary that follows each biblical passage launches your reflection on that passage and helps you begin to see its significance within the context of your contemporary experience. The questions following the commentary challenge you to understand the passage more fully and apply it to your own life. Space for writing after each question is ideal for personal study and also allows group participants to prepare for the weekly discussion. The prayer helps conclude your study each day by integrating your learning into your relationship with God.

The method of *Threshold Bible Study* is rooted in the ancient tradition of *lectio divina*, whereby studying the Bible becomes a means of deeper intimacy with God and a transformed life. Reading and interpreting the text (*lectio*) is followed by reflective meditation on its message (*meditatio*). This reading and reflecting flows into prayer from the heart (*oratio* and *contemplatio*). In this way, one listens to God through the Scripture and then responds to God in prayer.

This ancient method assures you that Bible study is a matter of both the mind and the heart. It is not just an intellectual exercise to learn more and be able to discuss the Bible with others. It is, more importantly, a transforming experience. Reflecting on God's word, guided by the Holy Spirit, illumines the mind with wisdom and stirs the heart with zeal.

Following the personal Bible study, *Threshold Bible Study* offers ways to extend personal *lectio divina* into a weekly conversation with others. This communal experience will allow participants to enhance their appreciation of the message and build up a spiritual community (*collatio*). The end result will be to increase not only individual faith but also faithful witness in the context of daily life (*operatio*).

When bringing *Threshold Bible Study* to a church community, try to make every effort to include as many people as possible. Many will want to study on their own; others will want to study with family, a group of friends, or a few work associates; some may want to commit themselves to share insights through a weekly conference call, daily text messaging, or an online social network; and others will want to gather weekly in established small groups.

By encouraging *Threshold Bible Study* and respecting the many ways people desire to make Bible study a regular part of their lives, you will widen the number of people in your church community who study the Bible regularly in whatever way they are able in their busy lives. Simply sign up people at the Sunday services and order bulk quantities for your church. Encourage people to follow the daily study as faithfully as they can. This encouragement can be through Sunday announcements, notices in parish publications, support on the church website, and other creative invitations and motivations.

Through the spiritual disciplines of Scripture reading, study, reflection, conversation, and prayer, *Threshold Bible Study* will help you experience God's grace more abundantly and root your life more deeply in Christ. The risen Jesus said: "Listen! I am standing at the door, knocking; if you hear my voice and open the door, I will come in to you and eat with you, and you with me" (Rev 3:20). Listen to the Word of God, open the door, and cross the threshold to an unimaginable dwelling with God!

SUGGESTIONS FOR INDIVIDUAL STUDY

• Make your Bible reading a time of prayer. Ask for God's guidance as you read the Scriptures.

• Try to study daily, or as often as possible according to the circumstances of your life.

• Read the Bible passage carefully, trying to understand both its meaning and its personal application as you read. Some persons find it helpful to read the passage aloud.

• Read the passage in another Bible translation. Each version adds to your understanding of the original text.

• Allow the commentary to help you comprehend and apply the scriptural text. The commentary is only a beginning, not the last word, on the meaning of the passage.

• After reflecting on each question, write out your responses. The very act of writing will help you clarify your thoughts, bring new insights, and amplify your understanding.

• As you reflect on your answers, think about how you can live God's word in the context of your daily life.

• Conclude each daily lesson by reading the prayer and continuing with your own prayer from the heart.

• Make sure your reflections and prayers are matters of both the mind and the heart. A true encounter with God's word is always a transforming experience.

• Choose a word or a phrase from the lesson to carry with you throughout the day as a reminder of your encounter with God's life-changing word.

• For additional insights and affirmation, share your learning experience with at least one other person whom you trust. The ideal way to share learning is in a small group that meets regularly.

SUGGESTIONS FOR GROUP STUDY

• Meet regularly; weekly is ideal. Try to be on time, and make attendance a high priority for the sake of the group. The average group meets for about an hour.

• Open each session with a prepared prayer, a song, or a reflection. Find some appropriate way to bring the group from the workaday world into a sacred time of graced sharing.

• If you have not been together before, name tags are very helpful as group members begin to become acquainted with one another.

• Spend the first session getting acquainted with one another, reading the Introduction aloud, and discussing the questions that follow.

• Appoint a group facilitator to provide guidance to the discussion. The role of facilitator may rotate among members each week. The facilitator simply keeps the discussion on track; each person shares responsibility for the group. There is no need for the facilitator to be a trained teacher.

• Try to study the six lessons on your own during the week. When you have done your own reflection and written your own answers, you will be better prepared to discuss the six scriptural lessons with the group. If you have not had an opportunity to study the passages during the week, meet with the group anyway to share support and insights.

• Participate in the discussion as much as you are able, offering your thoughts, insights, feelings, and decisions. You learn by sharing with others the fruits of your study.

• Be careful not to dominate the discussion. It is important that everyone in the group be offered an equal opportunity to share the results of their work. Try to link what you say to the comments of others so that the group remains on the topic.

• When discussing your own personal thoughts or feelings, use "I" language. Be as personal and honest as appropriate, and be very cautious about giving advice to others.

• Listen attentively to the other members of the group so as to learn from their insights. The words of the Bible affect each person in a different way, so a group provides a wealth of understanding for each member.

• Don't fear silence. Silence in a group is as important as silence in personal study. It allows individuals time to listen to the voice of God's Spirit and the opportunity to form their thoughts before they speak.

• Solicit several responses for each question. The thoughts of different people will build on the answers of others and will lead to deeper insights for all.

• Don't fear controversy. Differences of opinions are a sign of a healthy and honest group. If you cannot resolve an issue, continue on, agreeing to disagree. There is probably some truth in each viewpoint.

• Discuss the questions that seem most important for the group. There is no need to cover all the questions in the group session.

• Realize that some questions about the Bible cannot be resolved, even by experts. Don't get stuck on some issue for which there are no clear answers.

• Whatever is said in the group is said in confidence and should be regarded as such.

• Pray as a group in whatever way feels comfortable. Pray for the members of your group throughout the week.

Schedule for Group Study

Session 1: Introduction   Date: _____

Session 2: Lessons 1–6   Date: _____

Session 3: Lessons 7–12   Date: _____

Session 4: Lessons 13–18 Date: _____

Session 5: Lessons 19–24 Date: _____

Session 6: Lessons 25–30 Date: _____

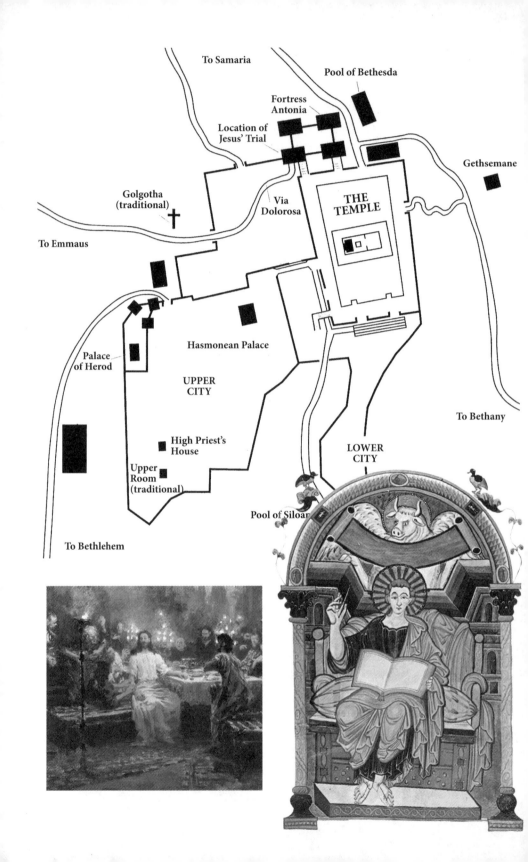

To Samaria

Pool of Bethesda

Fortress
Antonia

Location of
Jesus' Trial

Golgotha
(traditional)

THE
TEMPLE

Via
Dolorosa

Gethsemane

To Emmaus

Palace
of Herod

Hasmonean Palace

UPPER
CITY

To Bethany

LOWER
CITY

High Priest's
House

Upper
Room
(traditional)

Pool of Siloam

To Bethlehem

"Today, tomorrow, and the next day I must be on my way, because it is impossible for a prophet to be killed outside of Jerusalem." Luke 13:33

Jesus, the Compassionate Savior (Part 2)

At the end of Luke's gospel, we find the risen Jesus walking beside two of his disciples on the road to Emmaus, explaining the Scriptures to them. Later when these two disciples recognize Jesus at table with them, they reflect on their journey with him: "Were not our hearts burning within us while he talked to us on the road, while he was opening the Scriptures to us?" (24:32). As we read and reflect on the gospel of Luke, we are like those disciples on the road, as Jesus opens the Scriptures to us. The gospel is not just the historical record of what Jesus said and did. It is God's living word. Through this living word, Jesus speaks to us and reveals himself personally to us. Every phrase of the gospel is like a burning ember that has the potential to spark off the page and spread. We can expect our hearts to catch flame and burn with desire within us as we encounter Jesus through God's word. We can expect to hear him speak and to enlighten us as he opens the Scripture to us.

1

Luke is the only gospel to describe the preaching and teachings of Jesus as "the word of God" (5:1). Through the proclamation of the good news and the teachings of Jesus on the kingdom, God addresses his people. As the prophets spoke the word of God as recorded in the Scriptures of Israel, Jesus speaks so that people will hear the word of God. By comparing God's word to a seed in his parable of the sower (8:11), Jesus describes how God sows the word indiscriminately to all people, regardless of the condition of their lives. The task of the hearers of the word is to prepare the ground of their hearts to receive that word and allow it to take root, grow, and bear fruit. "Those who hear the word of God and do it" are those who are truly blessed (8:21; 11:28).

Through Luke's use of "the word of God" in the Acts of the Apostles to refer to the proclamation of the gospel by the early church, he links Jesus' preaching and teaching with that of the apostles. Indeed, he describes the mission of the church itself as the expansion and growth of the word of God (Acts 6:7; 8:14; 11:1; 12:24; 19:20). The prophets of old spoke God's word through the Spirit of God, that same Holy Spirit anointed Jesus to speak good news, and the Holy Spirit impelled the apostolic church to spread the word of God. In this same sense, the Torah and prophets of the Old Testament, the good news written by Luke and other evangelists, and the writings of the apostles and other ministers of the word in the New Testament are all inspired by the Holy Spirit to deliver the word of God to his people. Of all these sacred writings, we can truly proclaim, "The word of the Lord."

When these writings—"the law of Moses, the prophets, and the psalms" (24:44), and the gospel, the Acts, and the New Testament writings—are proclaimed in Christian liturgy, we can be assured that the risen Lord will open our minds to understand the Scriptures, just as he opened the minds of his disciples in Jerusalem (24:45). We can also rest with confidence that when we read the Scriptures in faith, we can expect our hearts to catch fire as we listen to God speak to us, just as the hearts of the disciples were burning within them as Jesus opened the Scriptures to them on the road to Emmaus. Our challenge is to take away the obstacles that prevent God's word from flourishing in our lives and to become disciples by listening, understanding, praying, and doing the word of God today.

Reflection and discussion

• What difference does it make in my study of the gospel to trust that it is God's living word?

• How does Luke convince his readers that all Scripture is inspired and speaks the word of God?

The Journey to Jerusalem

A large part of the second half of Luke's gospel consists of Jesus' journey to Jerusalem. Immediately after his Transfiguration, in which Moses and Elijah appeared in glory with Jesus and spoke about his "exodus" which he would accomplish in Jerusalem (9:31), Jesus "set his face to go to Jerusalem" (9:51). For the next ten chapters, Luke sets the teachings of Jesus within the context of this journey toward the city in which his death and resurrection will take place.

For Luke, Jerusalem is the goal of Jesus' mission, but the journey toward Jerusalem is also important. Luke presents the journey as a time of training and formation for his disciples, and in this section, Luke presents the bulk of Jesus' teaching. The road that Jesus followed is also the way his followers must travel. This kind of journey involves change and often hardships. Along the road Jesus clarifies the nature and demands of discipleship. Whereas in Jesus' ministry in Galilee, Jesus ministered primarily to the crowds, in his journey to Jerusalem, he speaks directly to his closest followers.

This part of the gospel contains lots of material that is found only in Luke. For example, through the marvelous parables of the good Samaritan, the rich fool, the barren fig tree, the lost coin, the prodigal son, the shrewd manager, and the rich man and Lazarus, Jesus illustrates for his disciples the ways of God's kingdom. Only in this gospel do we find Jesus' teachings on humility, on whom to invite for dinner, on seeking places of honor, and on the importance of counting the costs of discipleship. In this section, we find the story of Martha and Mary, which narrates the necessary dimensions of discipleship, and the description of Zacchaeus, who shows the only way a rich person can be a disciple. These accounts set Luke apart from the other three gospels and demonstrate how Jesus guides his disciples to become his church.

Using the journey as a theological metaphor, Luke invites his readers to accompany Jesus as he makes his way to Jerusalem. As the road to Jerusalem with Jesus was a time of training, preparation, and growth, so it is for us. Luke's readers travel into discipleship, learning what it means to follow Jesus and to participate in the reign of God. This journey of the spiritual life is the process of coming to know Jesus and learning to follow in his way. Along the way we must always be learning from Jesus, and we must continually be changing as we take his words to heart and follow in his way.

As Luke's readers, we know that our journey is also the journey of the church. In fact, throughout the Acts of the Apostles, Luke describes the church as "the Way," another term for expressing the journey of discipleship. And just as the disciples were accompanied by the Risen Jesus on their journey to Emmaus, we know that we are accompanied by the Lord and guided by the Holy Spirit.

Reflection and discussion

• What are some of the differences between the first and second half of Luke's gospel?

• In what way is my own growing relationship with Jesus like a road, way, or journey?

Compassion for the Lost and the Outcasts

One of the primary characteristics of Jesus' ministry, particularly as Luke presents it, is his care for those who are marginalized. This concern for those in need is presented in the inaugural scene in the synagogue at Nazareth in which Jesus presents his mission as the fulfillment of Isaiah's prophecy, bringing good news to the poor, release to captives, sight to the blind, and freedom to captives (4:18). The kingdom of God proclaimed by Jesus seems to be characterized by a reversal of the world's status quo. He announces that those who are poor, hungry, and weeping are the ones who are now blessed (6:20–21). In fact, those who are hated, excluded, reviled, and defamed because of following Jesus are those who should rejoice and leap for joy (6:22–23).

Luke's gospel has an especially large number of teachings about money, greed, and possessions. The parable of the rich fool indicates the absurdity of greed and the futility of accumulating possessions (12:16–21). The parable of the rich man and Lazarus emphasizes that the conditions of the poor man and the rich man are reversed at death. By including these parables, Luke is urging Theophilus and his other readers to be detached from material possessions and to share them with those in need.

Because of the way that Jesus attracted the marginalized, he became known as the one who welcomes and eats with tax collectors and sinners (15:1–2). Table fellowship is emphasized throughout Luke's gospel, and Jesus is depicted frequently as sharing meals with outcasts and peppering his teaching with references to food, banquets, and feasts. In the parable of the great banquet, expressing the inclusiveness and abundance of God's kingdom, the host sends his servant out into the city streets and back alleys of the town to invite the poor, disabled, and outcasts. When there is still room left at the table, he sends the servants out to the roads outside the town, encouraging everyone to attend from all directions (14:21–23).

Jesus' saving ministry is characterized by seeking out and finding the lost. His parables of the lost sheep, the lost coin, and the lost son illustrate the joy in heaven over a single sinner who repents. When Zacchaeus, the wealthy tax collector, becomes a disciple, Jesus declares that he himself has come "to seek out and to save the lost" (19:10). The point of each story is that God will go to great efforts and rejoice with great joy to find and restore a sinner to himself. Jesus shows himself to be a model for his disciples. Their mission, like that of Jesus, is to love people and draw them to God. They must reflect his concern and compassion, seeking out the lost and rejoicing with the heavens over every repentant sinner.

Jesus' care for the outcasts reaches its climax on the cross. The one who has sought to save sinners and seek out the lost throughout his life now asks God's forgiveness for his torturers (23:34). Jesus dies between two criminals, breathing his last with the same kind of people with whom he associated throughout his ministry. His words of mercy for his executioners seem to have inspired one of the two criminals crucified with him to repent and place his faith in Jesus. The words of Jesus, "Truly I tell you, today you will be with me in Paradise," solemnly declare that he can and does save those who turn to him. This reconciled criminal is the final example and result of Jesus' mission to call sinners to repentance, to seek out and save the lost.

Reflection and discussion

• In what ways does Luke emphasize the theme of reversal throughout his gospel?

• How might reflecting on Luke's gospel begin to change my priorities and the focus of my life?

The Holy Spirit: From the Gospel to Acts

At the beginning of Luke's gospel, the Holy Spirit comes upon Mary to give birth to Jesus. The Holy Spirit then animates and leads Jesus throughout the gospel's presentation of his saving ministry. At the beginning of Luke's second volume, the Acts of the Apostles, the Holy Spirit comes upon Mary and the apostles to give birth to the church. The same Holy Spirit then animates and leads the church throughout its foundational days as presented in Acts.

Throughout his life Jesus is filled with the Holy Spirit, empowering him to pray, to teach, and to heal. After his baptism by John, the Holy Spirit descends upon him in a manifest way (3:22), and then Jesus, "full of the Holy Spirit," is led by the Spirit into the wilderness (4:1). In the first act of his public ministry in Nazareth, Jesus declares that the words of the prophet are fulfilled: "The Spirit of the Lord is upon me" (4:18). Luke notes that Jesus "rejoiced in the Holy Spirit" as he prayed to his Father (10:21).

Luke highlights the role of the Holy Spirit in Jesus' life because he wants to emphasize the Spirit's role in the life of his readers. Jesus promises that the Father will "give the Holy Spirit to those who ask him" (11:13), and at the end of the gospel the risen Jesus instructs the apostles to wait in Jerusalem because he is sending upon them what the Father promised, the gift of the Holy Spirit to clothe them with power from on high (24:49). The Holy Spirit's guidance and empowerment in the life of Jesus sets the pattern for the Spirit's work in the lives of his followers.

In the Acts of the Apostles, the Holy Spirit animates the whole church in its evangelizing mission. In Acts, Luke mentions the Holy Spirit over fifty times, so much so that some have suggested that the book might be better entitled the Acts of the Holy Spirit. As we read and reflect on Luke's gospel, we should be aware that the same Spirit who breathed in Luke as he wrote lives today within the church and works within each of us as we read Luke's inspired work. God binds his own Spirit into these texts and meets us on the holy ground of these sacred pages.

Reflection and discussion

• What wisdom have I been given while studying the first part of Luke's gospel that will guide me as I continue?

• How do I expect the Holy Spirit to work within me during these weeks of reading and reflecting on Luke's gospel?

Prayer

Father of the poor and the lost, send your Holy Spirit upon me as I continue to listen to your word through the words and deeds of Jesus your Son. As I continue to study this gospel of Luke, help me to keep changing and growing as I learn and pray. May I follow Jesus along the journey to Jerusalem, listening to his teachings and learning from him the way of discipleship. As the risen Jesus opened the minds of his disciples to understand the Scriptures, let me trust in his guiding presence with me as I seek to understand your word in this holy gospel.

SUGGESTIONS FOR FACILITATORS, GROUP SESSION 1

1. If the group is meeting for the first time, or if there are newcomers joining the group, it is helpful to provide nametags.

2. Distribute the books to the members of the group.

3. You may want to ask the participants to introduce themselves and tell the group a bit about themselves.

4. Ask one or more of these introductory questions:
   • What drew you to join this group?
   • What is your biggest fear in beginning this Bible study?
   • How is beginning this study like a "threshold" for you?

5. You may want to pray this prayer as a group:

   Come upon us, Holy Spirit, to enlighten and guide us as we begin this study of Luke's gospel. You inspired the writers of the Scriptures to reveal your presence throughout the history of salvation. This inspired word has the power to convert our hearts and change our lives. Fill our hearts with desire, trust, and confidence as you shine the light of your truth within us. Motivate us to read the Scriptures, and give us a deeper love for God's word each day. Bless us during this session and throughout the coming week with the fire of your love.

6. Read the Introduction aloud, pausing at each question for discussion. Group members may wish to write the insights of the group as each question is discussed. Encourage several members of the group to respond to each question.

7. Don't feel compelled to finish the complete Introduction during the session. It is better to allow sufficient time to talk about the questions raised than to rush to the end. Group members may read any remaining sections on their own after the group meeting.

8. Instruct group members to read the first six lessons on their own during the six days before the next group meeting. They should write out their own answers to the questions as preparation for next week's group discussion.

9. Fill in the date for each group meeting under "Schedule for Group Study."

10. Conclude the session by praying aloud together the prayer at the end of the Introduction.

"I tell you, everyone who acknowledges me before others, the Son of Man also will acknowledge before the angels of God; but whoever denies me before others will be denied before the angels of God." Luke 12:8–9

Warnings against Hypocrisy, Denial, and Greed

LUKE 12:1–21 *¹Meanwhile, when the crowd gathered by the thousands, so that they trampled on one another, he began to speak first to his disciples, "Beware of the yeast of the Pharisees, that is, their hypocrisy. ²Nothing is covered up that will not be uncovered, and nothing secret that will not become known. ³Therefore whatever you have said in the dark will be heard in the light, and what you have whispered behind closed doors will be proclaimed from the housetops.*

⁴"I tell you, my friends, do not fear those who kill the body, and after that can do nothing more. ⁵But I will warn you whom to fear: fear him who, after he has killed, has authority to cast into hell. Yes, I tell you, fear him! ⁶Are not five sparrows sold for two pennies? Yet not one of them is forgotten in God's sight. ⁷But even the hairs of your head are all counted. Do not be afraid; you are of more value than many sparrows.

⁸"And I tell you, everyone who acknowledges me before others, the Son of Man also will acknowledge before the angels of God; ⁹but whoever denies me before others will be denied before the angels of God. ¹⁰*And everyone who speaks a word against the Son of Man will be forgiven; but whoever blasphemes against the Holy Spirit will not be forgiven.* ¹¹*When they bring you before the synagogues, the rulers, and the authorities, do not worry about how you are to defend yourselves or what you are to say;* ¹²*for the Holy Spirit will teach you at that very hour what you ought to say."*

¹³*Someone in the crowd said to him, "Teacher, tell my brother to divide the family inheritance with me."* ¹⁴*But he said to him, "Friend, who set me to be a judge or arbitrator over you?"* ¹⁵*And he said to them, "Take care! Be on your guard against all kinds of greed; for one's life does not consist in the abundance of possessions."* ¹⁶*Then he told them a parable: "The land of a rich man produced abundantly.* ¹⁷*And he thought to himself, 'What should I do, for I have no place to store my crops?'* ¹⁸*Then he said, 'I will do this: I will pull down my barns and build larger ones, and there I will store all my grain and my goods.* ¹⁹*And I will say to my soul, "Soul, you have ample goods laid up for many years; relax, eat, drink, be merry."'* ²⁰*But God said to him, 'You fool! This very night your life is being demanded of you. And the things you have prepared, whose will they be?'* ²¹*So it is with those who store up treasures for themselves but are not rich toward God."*

Jesus continues to travel with his disciples toward Jerusalem, offering them warnings and exhortations about the way they live. Although a huge crowd of thousands surrounds him, Jesus knows that his popularity is temporary, and he urges his disciples to be vigilant. He warns them not to become hypocritical like the Pharisees, pretending to be something they are not, hiding their failings behind a pious façade. Such a lifestyle is futile before God who sees all things (verses 2–3). Everything hidden will be uncovered, and everything that is secret will be revealed. For the hypocritical disciple, his words are a warning; for the genuine disciple, they are a reassurance.

Jesus is aware of the rising opposition he and his disciples face. Like the prophets before them, Jesus and his disciples face persecution and death. Calling his disciples "friends," Jesus urges them to be ready for martyrdom and not to fear those who can only kill their earthly bodies (verse 4). Rather, in a threefold repetitive warning, Jesus counsels his disciples to fear God, the only one who has sovereign care of their lives after physical death (verse 5).

Fear of God is not terror, but rather a respectful reverence for the authority of God, who will judge all people and determine their final destiny.

The Greek word for hell is "Gehenna," a steep ravine on the southern and western sides of Jerusalem where trash was discarded and burned. Other Jewish writings portray Gehenna as a place of fiery punishment and a symbol of God's judgment on the wicked. Jesus spoke of Gehenna as a gruesome contrast to the gracious care that God offers to those he remembers forever. If God does not neglect even the sparrows, the cheapest item sold in the market, how much more does he care for those he has created in his own image (verses 6–7).

Genuine disciples bear witness to Jesus before other people. At the time of judgment, Jesus will testify on behalf of those who have testified on behalf of him (verse 8). In times of persecution, some will speak a word against Jesus, as Peter will do before the authorities in Jerusalem, but they will be forgiven when they repent (verse 10). But when people "blaspheme against the Holy Spirit," denying the power of God's Spirit within them and obstinately rejecting their allegiance to Jesus, they reject their ability to be forgiven. When disciples are brought before Jewish and Roman authorities, they should trust in God and not worry about how they will defend themselves (verse 11). Rather than speaking against the work of the Holy Spirit, they will allow the Spirit to speak within them. The Holy Spirit will give them the words to say, so that they can bear witness to Jesus. Luke will show us examples of the trust and testimony of Peter, Stephen, and Paul in the Acts of the Apostles.

When someone in the crowd asks Jesus to step into a family dispute about an inheritance, Jesus takes the occasion to teach about the danger of focusing on material wealth. He warns them about greed, and he stresses that "life does not consist in the abundance of possessions" (verse 15). No one can pull a U-Haul behind the hearse. A truly rich life is one oriented toward God and focused on his will.

Jesus reinforces his teaching with a parable about possessions. The rich man with the bountiful harvest has no place to store his abundance, so he decides to expand his storage capacity. The parable is full of the pronoun "I," and the man's wealth is described as "my crops," "my barns," "my grain," and "my goods" (verses 17–19). His future perspective is self-centered and self-indulgent. With no thought of his responsibilities before God or the needs of others, the rich man's security is fleeting. His wealth cannot last and his greed leaves him empty when God demands his life. Because the man trusted in his possessions instead of in God, he is impoverished at his death in what matters to God.

Reflection and discussion

• What is a respectful "fear" of God (verse 5)? In what sense does Jesus tell us, "Do not be afraid" of God (verse 7)?

• What is the difference between the plans of the selfish rich man in the parable and the prudent plans we must make to provide for our family and retirement?

• What should I include in my investment portfolio in order to become rich in what matters to God?

Prayer

Jesus, my Friend, send your Holy Spirit so that I will have the courage to bear witness to you, even when I am overwhelmed by insecurity and fear. Free me from the seduction of greed, and help me to store up genuine riches in your sight.

"Blessed are those slaves whom the master finds alert when he comes; truly I tell you, he will fasten his belt and have them sit down to eat, and he will come and serve them." Luke 12:37

Exhortation to Be Trustful, Watchful, and Faithful

LUKE 12:22–48 *²²He said to his disciples, "Therefore I tell you, do not worry about your life, what you will eat, or about your body, what you will wear. ²³For life is more than food, and the body more than clothing. ²⁴Consider the ravens: they neither sow nor reap, they have neither storehouse nor barn, and yet God feeds them. Of how much more value are you than the birds! ²⁵And can any of you by worrying add a single hour to your span of life? ²⁶If then you are not able to do so small a thing as that, why do you worry about the rest? ²⁷Consider the lilies, how they grow: they neither toil nor spin; yet I tell you, even Solomon in all his glory was not clothed like one of these. ²⁸But if God so clothes the grass of the field, which is alive today and tomorrow is thrown into the oven, how much more will he clothe you—you of little faith! ²⁹And do not keep striving for what you are to eat and what you are to drink, and do not keep worrying. ³⁰For it is the nations of the world that strive after all these things, and your Father knows that you need them. ³¹Instead, strive for his kingdom, and these things will be given to you as well.*

³²"Do not be afraid, little flock, for it is your Father's good pleasure to give you the kingdom. ³³Sell your possessions, and give alms. Make purses for yourselves that do not wear out, an unfailing treasure in heaven, where no thief comes near and no moth destroys. ³⁴For where your treasure is, there your heart will be also.

³⁵"Be dressed for action and have your lamps lit; ³⁶be like those who are waiting for their master to return from the wedding banquet, so that they may open the door for him as soon as he comes and knocks. ³⁷Blessed are those slaves whom the master finds alert when he comes; truly I tell you, he will fasten his belt and have them sit down to eat, and he will come and serve them. ³⁸If he comes during the middle of the night, or near dawn, and finds them so, blessed are those slaves.

³⁹"But know this: if the owner of the house had known at what hour the thief was coming, he would not have let his house be broken into. ⁴⁰You also must be ready, for the Son of Man is coming at an unexpected hour."

⁴¹Peter said, "Lord, are you telling this parable for us or for everyone?" ⁴²And the Lord said, "Who then is the faithful and prudent manager whom his master will put in charge of his slaves, to give them their allowance of food at the proper time? ⁴³Blessed is that slave whom his master will find at work when he arrives. ⁴⁴Truly I tell you, he will put that one in charge of all his possessions. ⁴⁵But if that slave says to himself, 'My master is delayed in coming,' and if he begins to beat the other slaves, men and women, and to eat and drink and get drunk, ⁴⁶the master of that slave will come on a day when he does not expect him and at an hour that he does not know, and will cut him in pieces, and put him with the unfaithful. ⁴⁷That slave who knew what his master wanted, but did not prepare himself or do what was wanted, will receive a severe beating. ⁴⁸But the one who did not know and did what deserved a beating will receive a light beating. From everyone to whom much has been given, much will be required; and from the one to whom much has been entrusted, even more will be demanded."

Jesus continues to teach his disciples how to trust in God's care for them. He urges them not to worry about such things as food and clothing because life is so much more than these necessities. If disciples are overly anxious about these matters, they will neglect and even miss life's most important concerns. The security that we often look for in food and clothing can be found only in God. When we focus on striving for his kingdom, we can trust in God to provide what we need.

Jesus offers a series of illustrations from nature that emphasize the point that disciples need not worry because they can rely on God's gracious care.

The ravens don't fret about growing crops or storing them, but God supplies all of their needs through the provisions of nature. Jesus reminds his disciples how valuable they are to God who will surely provide for them. Worrying is a completely useless activity, wasting energy and adding nothing to our lives. In fact, we know today that it lessens both the length and the quality of life. Similarly, the lilies don't fuss about their garments and they neither spin nor weave. Yet, they are more splendidly clothed than Solomon, the wealthiest of Israel's kings. Likewise, God provides for the grass of the field, which thrives today and is fuel for cooking fires tomorrow. If God cares for the birds, the lilies, and even the grass, surely God will provide abundantly for the disciples of Jesus.

When Jesus sent his chosen disciples out on mission, he commanded them to travel without money or provisions, trusting in God's care and the hospitality of people along the way. Jesus was offering his disciples an opportunity to strengthen their faith in God. Undue worry and anxious striving is characteristic of the human condition in the world, but it is not necessary for disciples whose heavenly Father hears their prayers and knows their needs (verses 29–31). Jesus teaches his disciples that they need not make striving for survival their goal in life, but that they must strive for God's kingdom and live under God's reign. By putting first things first, they can live in the hands of their Father and enjoy the quality of life that lasts forever.

Because the Father graciously offers the kingdom to the disciples of Jesus, they can live free from fear and unattached to material possessions (verses 32–33). Living in this way enables disciples to care for the needs of others and accumulate nonperishable, everlasting treasure. Attachment to God, rather than to the things of earth, enables disciples to give over all for God's service and to live in readiness for the final coming of Jesus and the culmination of the kingdom.

Jesus offers images and parables to express the preparedness and watchfulness he desires for his disciples (verses 35–36). He tells them to cinch up their long robes with a belt so that they can move swiftly and to light their lamps so that they can see in the dark. The parable compares the disciples to servants awaiting their master's return. Even though he might come in the middle of the night, as unexpectedly as a thief, they must be ready to open the house to him and be at his service. Yet, in the words of a beatitude, Jesus reverses the images of master and servant for those who are prepared for his coming (verse

37). The master will cinch up his robe, inviting his servants to recline at table, and then he will serve them at the great banquet of God's kingdom.

In the final exhortation to his disciples, Jesus urges them to be faithful and prudent managers over God's household while the master is away (verses 42-43). Those who faithfully carry out their duties will be blessed with greater responsibility and service when the Lord returns. But those who fail in their responsibilities, taking advantage of their position, will be harshly judged. The servant-leaders of Christ's church must serve with one eye looking for Jesus' return and the other searching for ways of carrying out their responsibilities, knowing that they must give an account of their service.

Reflection and discussion

• Why do I tend to look for security in the material things of life? What can I do to remind myself that living is more than having?

• How can following the teachings of Jesus increase both the length and the quality of my life? In what ways do I rely on God's care?

Prayer

Father in heaven, I desire to live with my eyes fixed on your kingdom and to walk each day in its light. Help me to live free from anxiety and fear, waiting in joyful expectation for the coming of our Lord, Jesus Christ.

"You know how to interpret the appearance of earth and sky,
but why do you not know how to interpret the present time?" Luke 12:56

Knowing the Nature of the Time

LUKE 12:49–59 ⁴⁹*"I came to bring fire to the earth, and how I wish it were already kindled!* ⁵⁰*I have a baptism with which to be baptized, and what stress I am under until it is completed!* ⁵¹*Do you think that I have come to bring peace to the earth? No, I tell you, but rather division!* ⁵²*From now on five in one household will be divided, three against two and two against three;* ⁵³*they will be divided:*

father against son
and son against father,
mother against daughter
and daughter against mother,
mother-in-law against her daughter-in-law
and daughter-in-law against mother-in-law."

⁵⁴*He also said to the crowds, "When you see a cloud rising in the west, you immediately say, 'It is going to rain'; and so it happens.* ⁵⁵*And when you see the south wind blowing, you say, 'There will be scorching heat'; and it happens.* ⁵⁶*You hypocrites! You know how to interpret the appearance of earth and sky, but why do you not know how to interpret the present time?*

⁵⁷*"And why do you not judge for yourselves what is right?* ⁵⁸*Thus, when you*

18

go with your accuser before a magistrate, on the way make an effort to settle the case, or you may be dragged before the judge, and the judge hand you over to the officer, and the officer throw you in prison. ⁵⁹I tell you, you will never get out until you have paid the very last penny."

A fter Jesus urges his disciples to live in fearless trust and admonishes them to be prepared for his glorious return, he turns to his present ministry and his desire to complete it. Focusing briefly on three different themes in these three paragraphs, he shows his audience "how to interpret the present time" (verse 56).

"I came to bring fire to the earth" reads like a mission statement of Jesus. In addition to his mission of bringing good news to the poor, sight to the blind, freedom for the oppressed, and proclaiming a year of the Lord's favor (4:18–19), he has come to set the earth on fire. The image of fire can represent different things in the biblical literature. The prophets associated fire with God's word. Jeremiah speaks: "Is not my word like fire? says the Lord" (Jer 23:29). Sirach says, "Then Elijah arose, a prophet like fire, and his word burned like a torch" (Sir 48:1). Fire is also an image in the Hebrew Scriptures of God's refining and purifying his people, as fire separates the impurities from precious metals. The mission of Jesus is to release people from the oppression of evil, to proclaim God's word of repentance and good news, and to purify them with a refiner's fire, so that they will shine as God's precious treasure. Jesus expresses his desire that his mission be under way: "How I wish it were already kindled!" But before his mission can be accomplished, Jesus must be "baptized" in suffering, that is, plunged into his agony and death. Through the baptism of his passion, Jesus will baptize God's people "with the Holy Spirit and fire" (3:16).

One of the results of Jesus' mission is "division" among people, penetrating even the most intimate level of relationships within families (verse 51). Of course, as Jesus has promised, "peace" will come to those who respond to the gospel he brings. To those he forgives and heals, Jesus says, "Go in peace" (7:50; 8:48), and he sends out his disciples to proclaim, "Peace to this house" (10:5). But this peace is tied to the message of salvation and is given to those who respond positively to this gift. Jesus' offer of salvation contains the choice between aligning with God's kingdom or standing against it.

Jesus' warning of separation along generational lines within families alludes to the words of Micah. The prophet laments the divisions between sons and fathers, daughters and mothers, and daughters-in-law and mothers-in-law (Mic 7:6). The covenant bonds of fidelity have been broken, shattering all relationships within families and community. Micah says that God's people are like a brier with no ripe figs to be found (Mic 7:1), an image that Jesus will also use in his teaching (13:6). Yet, hope is not lost and God continues his saving work, until God's people turn to him and say, "I will look to the Lord, I will wait for the God of my salvation" (Mic 7:7). Likewise, Jesus does not come to break up families, but divisions arise because of the different responses people make to him. But God continues to work among his people, seeking to bring them to the peace and salvation he desires for all.

Jesus chides the people for their inability to determine the nature of the events happening around them. While they can easily discern the signs that predict the coming weather, they are unable to recognize what God is doing in their midst (verses 54–56). Jesus has provided much evidence of God's saving activity, but the people have not responded well and do not perceive that Jesus is establishing the reign of God.

Considering the urgency of the present moment and the signs of the times around them, Jesus urges the people to take the right course of action. With the parable of the debtor, he insists that they settle their accounts with God. It is better to settle one's debts than to go to court, have one's guilt exposed, and be forced to serve time in prison until the debt is paid (verse 58). The point Jesus makes is that we should respond to God's call and repent now, before it is too late. The final verse illustrates the hopeless situation of one who fails to respond to God's offer and repent.

Reflection and discussion

• What are some of the possible meanings of Jesus' statement: "I came to bring fire to the earth, and how I wish it were already kindled"? What are his words saying to me?

• What are some of the divisions that the gospel has brought to society, communities, and families?

• What are some of the signs pointing to what Jesus is doing in the world and in my own life today?

• What is the meaning of Jesus' parable of the debtor (verses 58–59)? What should I do to settle my account with God?

Prayer

Come, Holy Spirit, fill the hearts of your faithful, and enkindle in them the fire of your love. Guide me to see and discern the signs of the times. Give me a repentant heart so that I can know your peace and salvation.

"A man had a fig tree planted in his vineyard; and he came looking for fruit on it and found none." Luke 13:6

God's Patient Call to Repentance

LUKE 13:1–9 ¹*At that very time there were some present who told him about the Galileans whose blood Pilate had mingled with their sacrifices. ²He asked them, "Do you think that because these Galileans suffered in this way they were worse sinners than all other Galileans? ³No, I tell you; but unless you repent, you will all perish as they did. ⁴Or those eighteen who were killed when the tower of Siloam fell on them—do you think that they were worse offenders than all the others living in Jerusalem? ⁵No, I tell you; but unless you repent, you will all perish just as they did."*

⁶Then he told this parable: "A man had a fig tree planted in his vineyard; and he came looking for fruit on it and found none. ⁷So he said to the gardener, 'See here! For three years I have come looking for fruit on this fig tree, and still I find none. Cut it down! Why should it be wasting the soil?' ⁸He replied, 'Sir, let it alone for one more year, until I dig around it and put manure on it. ⁹If it bears fruit next year, well and good; but if not, you can cut it down.'"

Continuing the theme of "how to interpret the present time" (12:56), Jesus uses two recent tragedies to emphasize the need for repentance. First, some in the crowd bring up an incident in which some Galileans, as they were coming to Jerusalem to offer their sacrifices, were put to death by the troops of Pontius Pilate. An attack like this in the area of the temple must have created quite a stir and raised passions, and Jesus is asked to comment on it. But instead of inciting hostility, Jesus uses the opportunity to offer a reflection on their relationship with God. Second, Jesus brings up the tragic deaths of eighteen people in Jerusalem who died when a tower fell upon them. Again, Jesus uses the incident as a wake-up call, an occasion for people to consider the signs of the times and the need to get right with God.

To each tragedy, Jesus asks whether the victims were worse sinners than others. Jesus raises what would be the typical conclusion, only to reject each of his own questions with an emphatic "No." Rather, Jesus warns them about the fragile nature of life and the tragic end that faces everyone who fails to repent. The timing and circumstances of death are not so important when compared to the woes that come to those who fail to respond to God's saving work. Jesus concludes with the lesson offered by these tragic deaths: "Unless you repent, you will perish as they did." This repentance that Jesus continually urges is a change of course in one's life, reforming one's thinking and behavior, and orienting oneself to God.

Jesus' parable of the fig tree emphasizes the immediate danger that faces his whole audience. The owner of the vineyard ordered that a fig tree be cut down because it had not borne fruit for three years. He knew that the unproductive tree was taking nutrients from the other plants in the garden and taking up space where other vines and fruit trees could be planted. The image of the barren fig tree portrays the people of Israel who have not generated any spiritual produce for a long time. The owner's displeasure expresses God's evaluation of his people. But the gardener pleaded for the tree, asking the owner to give him one more year to carefully nurture the tree so that it will bear fruit.

The parable is left open-ended. It expresses God's patience with his people, graciously allowing a last chance to bear fruit, despite a history of unfruitfulness. Yet, it also conveys the urgency of the times. The time for repentance is short and the stakes are high. The image recalls the exhortation of John the Baptist, "Bear fruit worthy of your repentance," as well as his urgent warning that the ax lies at the root of the tree (3:8-9). God is sending his word through Jesus and desires that his people receive the word in good soil, so that they will "hear the word, hold it fast in an honest and good heart, and bear fruit with patient endurance" (8:15). The outcome is uncertain. Now is the time to repent and be fruitful.

Reflection and discussion

• Is there a connection between sin and suffering? How do I understand lives cut short by man-made or accidental tragedies?

• In what ways does God give special care and extra chances to those who fail to respond to his saving grace?

• What would I do if I knew I had one year to prepare myself to "bear fruit"? What fruit would I like to be producing at this time next year?

Prayer

Divine Teacher, you show me how to trust in your merciful love. I am grateful for the ways that you care for me and for your patience toward me. Continue teaching me how to reform my life and turn it completely toward you.

"What is the kingdom of God like?
And to what should I compare it?" Luke 13:18

Understanding the Kingdom of God

LUKE 13:10–21 [10]*Now he was teaching in one of the synagogues on the sabbath.* [11]*And just then there appeared a woman with a spirit that had crippled her for eighteen years. She was bent over and was quite unable to stand up straight.* [12]*When Jesus saw her, he called her over and said, "Woman, you are set free from your ailment."* [13]*When he laid his hands on her, immediately she stood up straight and began praising God.* [14]*But the leader of the synagogue, indignant because Jesus had cured on the sabbath, kept saying to the crowd, "There are six days on which work ought to be done; come on those days and be cured, and not on the sabbath day."* [15]*But the Lord answered him and said, "You hypocrites! Does not each of you on the sabbath untie his ox or his donkey from the manger, and lead it away to give it water?* [16]*And ought not this woman, a daughter of Abraham whom Satan bound for eighteen long years, be set free from this bondage on the sabbath day?"* [17]*When he said this, all his opponents were put to shame; and the entire crowd was rejoicing at all the wonderful things that he was doing.*

[18]*He said therefore, "What is the kingdom of God like? And to what should I compare it?* [19]*It is like a mustard seed that someone took and sowed in the gar-*

den; it grew and became a tree, and the birds of the air made nests in its branches."

20 And again he said, "To what should I compare the kingdom of God? 21 It is like yeast that a woman took and mixed in with three measures of flour until all of it was leavened."

A s a general rule, people do not come to Jesus for healing on the Sabbath, because they know that travel and labor are forbidden on the day of rest. If they are listening to Jesus in the synagogue on the Sabbath, they wait until sundown to approach him with their needs (4:40). Yet, on the several occasions when we see him heal on the Sabbath, Jesus himself takes the initiative. It seems, for some reason, that Jesus even prefers to heal on the Sabbath.

Here Jesus takes notice of the woman who is bent over and unable to stand erect. We learn that the woman is crippled because she has been held in bondage by Satan for eighteen long years (verses 11, 16). Jesus initiates the healing by calling her over and then proclaims that she is "set free" from her ailment. As Jesus lays his hands on her, she stands up straight and gives praise to God. Her healing is described as her liberation from bondage. In response to the synagogue leader who told the crowd to come for healing on any of the other six days of the week, but not on the Sabbath, Jesus makes a reasonable argument. If it is permissible to untie an ox or donkey on the Sabbath, how much more ought this woman be loosed from her bondage. Jesus shows that her healing is an act of liberation, recalling his mission stated earlier in another synagogue that he is to "proclaim release to the captives" and to "let the oppressed go free" (4:18).

Jesus heals on the Sabbath not to enrage the religious leaders, but to highlight the Sabbath-significance of his mission. The purpose of the Sabbath is the remembrance of the liberation of God's people from their bondage. As stated in the Torah, "Remember that you were a slave in the land of Egypt, and the Lord your God brought you out from there with a mighty hand and an outstretched arm; therefore the Lord your God commanded you to keep the Sabbath day" (Deut 5:15). Since the Sabbath is a remembrance of the exodus, what better day to free the captives and let them enjoy rest from their servitude.

As Luke's gospel demonstrates, Jesus is leading a new exodus. As the Lord of the Sabbath, he has come to liberate God's people from all the powers of evil that hold them bound. Jesus' deeds on the Sabbath, far from being opposed to the Sabbath rest, completely support the truest purpose of the Sabbath.

Despite the powerful deeds of Jesus, his ministry does not look like the overwhelming and decisive deliverance of God's people, as many had expected. The coming of God's kingdom, rather, is a gradual process of growth that will later culminate in a total presence. Like a small mustard seed that will grow into a sapling and eventually into a tree where the birds can build their nests, the kingdom will develop and produce a place of shelter and life for all (verse 19). Like a bit of yeast mixed in with the flour, the kingdom appears insignificant now, but will eventually expand and permeate the world (verse 21). Although the kingdom appears deceptively impotent in its present form, its inherent power presses it to grow, spread, and transform God's creation.

These two parables call disciples to trust in the way God is developing the kingdom in the world. In its early phases, God's reign is especially active in the church, the community of believers in Christ. As the living sacrament of God's kingdom, the church is called to express the redeeming presence of Christ and God's forgiving and healing love in the world. These parables give hope to the community of disciples and all readers of Luke's gospel, who form the church and participate in God's development of his reign in the world.

Reflection and discussion

• Why does Jesus take the initiative to heal on the Sabbath despite the objections of the synagogue leaders?

•What is the bondage from which God wishes to liberate his people today? How can I be an instrument of that release?

• What is the relationship of the church to the kingdom of God? Why are the images of the mustard seed and the yeast helpful images for believers today?

• What does the image of leaven in the dough express about how God is at work in the world today?

Prayer

Lord of the Sabbath, thank you for looking on your people with compassion and freeing them from the bonds of suffering, sin, and evil. Help me to see the growth of your kingdom in small ways in the world today, as I await the full coming of your reign in glory.

"Jerusalem, Jerusalem, the city that kills the prophets
and stones those who are sent to it!" Luke 13:34

On the Way to Jerusalem

LUKE 13:22–35 ²²*Jesus went through one town and village after another, teaching as he made his way to Jerusalem.* ²³*Someone asked him, "Lord, will only a few be saved?" He said to them,* ²⁴*"Strive to enter through the narrow door; for many, I tell you, will try to enter and will not be able.* ²⁵*When once the owner of the house has got up and shut the door, and you begin to stand outside and to knock at the door, saying, 'Lord, open to us,' then in reply he will say to you, 'I do not know where you come from.'* ²⁶*Then you will begin to say, 'We ate and drank with you, and you taught in our streets.'* ²⁷*But he will say, 'I do not know where you come from; go away from me, all you evildoers!'* ²⁸*There will be weeping and gnashing of teeth when you see Abraham and Isaac and Jacob and all the prophets in the kingdom of God, and you yourselves thrown out.* ²⁹*Then people will come from east and west, from north and south, and will eat in the kingdom of God.* ³⁰*Indeed, some are last who will be first, and some are first who will be last."*

³¹*At that very hour some Pharisees came and said to him, "Get away from here, for Herod wants to kill you."* ³²*He said to them, "Go and tell that fox for me, 'Listen, I am casting out demons and performing cures today and tomorrow, and on the third day I finish my work.* ³³*Yet today, tomorrow, and the next day I must be on my way, because it is impossible for a prophet to be killed outside of Jerusalem.'* ³⁴*Jerusalem, Jerusalem, the city that kills the prophets and stones those who are sent to it! How often have I desired to gather your children togeth-*

29

er as a hen gathers her brood under her wings, and you were not willing! [35]*See, your house is left to you. And I tell you, you will not see me until the time comes when you say, 'Blessed is the one who comes in the name of the Lord.'"*

Throughout his mission, Jesus has proclaimed in word and deed the good news of the kingdom of God. He continues to do so, teaching in one town and village after another, as he steadily makes his way toward Jerusalem. Alternating between messages of warning and hope, Jesus continually asserts that the time is short and that people must respond to God's offer of the kingdom before it is too late.

In response to a question about the number of those who will be saved, Jesus offers the image of the narrow door. This is the door that leads into the kingdom of God where the messianic banquet is served. Jesus teaches that one's Jewish heritage and ethnic identity are not enough to be numbered among those who will dine in God's kingdom. Jesus urges his listeners to "strive to enter through the narrow door" (verse 24). The image is one of struggling to enter rather than strolling in. Many who expect to enter will be unable to do so. Even though the invitation is God's gift, the effort to enter includes repentance, turning from wrongdoing, and a positive and trusting response to what God is doing in Jesus. Furthermore, Jesus states that the door will only be open for a short time. Because the owner of the house will shut the door after the banquet begins, it is urgent that Jesus' listeners open their hearts to God's offer of life.

Many who try to enter the kingdom will wail and rage that they are turned away, especially when they see people from throughout the whole world dining in the kingdom with the ancient patriarchs and prophets of Israel (verses 28–29). Those who are shut out protest that they ate and drank with Jesus and listened to him teach in their streets. But the Lord of the kingdom declares that he does not recognize them because they did not inwardly respond to him. Outward contact with Jesus does not save. Jesus urges his listeners to ask, not how many will be saved, but whether they themselves will be saved. Only a genuine relationship with Jesus and acceptance of his word leads through the door to eternal life.

As Jesus continues on his way to Jerusalem, he knows that he faces certain death. Even when he is warned that Herod and other officials are seeking his life, he states his determination to finish his work in Jerusalem (verse 32). He knows that the end of his life is near, and he also knows that the time of the open door is short and that it is closing for many in Israel. Jesus is described as a prophet lamenting the rejection of their Messiah by many in Israel (verse 34). Jerusalem is the city that kills its prophets and stones its messengers. This is the place where Jesus too must suffer and die.

Jesus offers a tender image to express how much God has longed to care for the people of Israel, gathering them for nurturance and protection, "as a hen gathers her brood under her wings." Yet, God can only guide and care for his people to the degree that they open themselves to his saving care. Jesus painfully states, "you were not willing!" Tragically, Jerusalem will soon kill another messenger, its own Messiah, and miss its opportunity for deliverance. Yet, in the final scope of history, Israel will indeed acknowledge Jesus as "the one who comes in the name of the Lord," when he returns in glory at the end of the age.

Reflection and discussion

• What does Jesus intend to express through his image of the narrow door? Why doesn't God just widen the doorway?

• Why do some not enter the door of God's kingdom when God has issued an open invitation to all?

• Who are those who seem to be last and far away from God's kingdom but end up being near and enter the banquet? Why are some who seem first and near end up being last and rejected from the kingdom?

•How do I align the goals of my life with God's will for me?

• What does the image of a hen gathering her chicks under her wings express to me about God's care?

Prayer

Jesus Messiah, I want you to be the Lord of my life. Teach me to make your kingdom the top priority of my life and to align the goals of my life with your will for me. Guide me through the open door, and help me be willing to enter into the banquet of your life.

SUGGESTIONS FOR FACILITATORS, GROUP SESSION 2

1. If there are newcomers who were not present for the first group session, introduce them now.

2. You may want to pray this prayer as a group:

Father of our Lord Jesus Christ, as we travel with your Son along the road to Jerusalem, help us avoid anxiety, greed, and selfish concerns, and keep us trustful, watchful, and faithful. Jesus has come to light a fire on the earth and to enflame our hearts with a desire for your kingdom. As you have loosened our bondage to suffering, sin, and evil, may we live in joyful hope for the gradual but certain growth of your reign in the world. As we continue to study, reflect, and pray with the gospel of Luke, send us your Spirit to guide and direct us.

3. Ask one or more of the following questions:
   • What was your biggest challenge in Bible study over this past week?
   • What did you learn about yourself this week?

4. Discuss together lessons 1 through 6. Assuming that group members have read the Scripture and commentary during the week, there is no need to read it aloud. As you review each lesson, you might want to briefly summarize the Scripture passages of each lesson and ask the group what stands out most clearly from the commentary.

5. Choose one or more of the questions for reflection and discussion from each lesson to talk over as a group. You may want to ask group members which question was most challenging or helpful to them as you review each lesson.

6. Keep the discussion moving, but don't rush the discussion in order to complete more questions. Allow time for the questions that provoke the most discussion.

7. Instruct group members to complete lessons 7 through 12 on their own during the six days before the next group meeting. They should write out their own answers to the questions as preparation for next week's group discussion.

8. Conclude by praying aloud together the prayer at the end of lesson 6, or any other prayer you choose.

"When you give a banquet, invite the poor, the crippled, the lame, and the blind. And you will be blessed, because they cannot repay you." Luke 14:13–14

Lessons at the Dining Table

LUKE 14:1–14 ¹*On one occasion when Jesus was going to the house of a leader of the Pharisees to eat a meal on the sabbath, they were watching him closely.* ²*Just then, in front of him, there was a man who had dropsy.* ³*And Jesus asked the lawyers and Pharisees, "Is it lawful to cure people on the sabbath, or not?"* ⁴*But they were silent. So Jesus took him and healed him, and sent him away.* ⁵*Then he said to them, "If one of you has a child or an ox that has fallen into a well, will you not immediately pull it out on a sabbath day?"* ⁶*And they could not reply to this.*

⁷*When he noticed how the guests chose the places of honor, he told them a parable.* ⁸*"When you are invited by someone to a wedding banquet, do not sit down at the place of honor, in case someone more distinguished than you has been invited by your host;* ⁹*and the host who invited both of you may come and say to you, 'Give this person your place,' and then in disgrace you would start to take the lowest place.* ¹⁰*But when you are invited, go and sit down at the lowest place, so that when your host comes, he may say to you, 'Friend, move up higher'; then you will be honored in the presence of all who sit at the table with you.* ¹¹*For all who exalt themselves will be humbled, and those who humble themselves will be exalted."*

¹²*He said also to the one who had invited him, "When you give a luncheon or a dinner, do not invite your friends or your brothers or your relatives or rich*

neighbors, in case they may invite you in return, and you would be repaid. [13]*But when you give a banquet, invite the poor, the crippled, the lame, and the blind.* [14]*And you will be blessed, because they cannot repay you, for you will be repaid at the resurrection of the righteous."*

This scene of Jesus dining at the house of a leader of the Pharisees, like many other episodes in his journey to Jerusalem, is found only in Luke's gospel. Meal settings are common in Luke's work, and Jesus is described as eating with everyone, whether they be tax collectors, or sinners, or religious leaders. The context here is a Sabbath meal, prepared the previous day so that the Sabbath is preserved as a day of rest. Meals were often served after synagogue services, and the discussion of biblical topics was frequently carried over from the service.

Seeing a man who has dropsy, a condition in which body tissue swells due to fluid retention, Jesus asks whether or not it is lawful to cure people on the Sabbath. He places the lawyers and the Pharisees in a difficult position. Their tradition taught that medical procedures for non-life-threatening conditions may not be performed on the Sabbath, but that life-threatening conditions may be treated. Since the man with dropsy, as well as the man with the withered hand (6:6) and the bent-over woman (13:11), all have conditions that could be treated any other day of the week, they believe that such healing is forbidden on the Sabbath. Yet, these legal experts remain silent, fearing that they would be seen as standing against doing good and showing compassion if they ruled against the healing.

So Jesus, the Lord of the Sabbath and the messianic liberator of God's people, heals the man and sets him free. Knowing what the Pharisees and lawyers were thinking, Jesus continues on the offensive and asks them what they would do if they had a child, or even an ox, that had fallen into a well. Surely they would provide such basic assistance and rescue on the Sabbath. Again the religious leaders fall silent, unable to respond. Jesus' intention is not to debate the fine points of the law, but to open their hearts to what God is doing through him. He is setting free those in bondage so that all can enter the door of God's kingdom and share in God's banquet forever.

The meal with the Pharisees provides Jesus an opportunity to continue teaching about God's kingdom. When Jesus notices the guests seeking the places of honor in the dining room, he teaches about the humility required for entering the kingdom. In the form of a parable, he shows that those who take the lowest place are those who know their unworthiness and look to God's grace to move up higher, while those who exalt themselves and assume the highest places for themselves will be humiliated. Again we see the theme of divine reversal in which the proud are humbled and the humble are exalted.

Jesus also takes the occasion to teach about hospitality and generosity in God's kingdom which his disciples should imitate. Rather than inviting people who are able to repay hospitality, a host of a banquet should invite "the poor, the crippled, the lame, and the blind." Hospitality and generosity are genuine when no motive exists besides giving. Again we see that humility and openness to all people are key principles taught by Jesus to those seeking to follow him.

Reflection and discussion

• What does Jesus' willingness to dine with the Pharisees, despite their opposition to him, show me about the character of Jesus? What characteristic is he calling me to imitate?

• What are the principal considerations of Jesus when deciding what to do and not to do on the Sabbath?

Prayer

Lord Jesus, you have invited me to the banquet of your kingdom, even though I can never repay your invitation. Give me humility and generosity so that I can share your boundless hospitality with those who cannot repay me.

LESSON 8   **SESSION 3**

> "At the time for the dinner he sent his slave to say to those
> who had been invited, 'Come; for everything is ready now.'
> But they all alike began to make excuses." Luke 14:17–18

Counting the Costs of Commitment

LUKE 14:15–33 [15]*One of the dinner guests, on hearing this, said to him,
"Blessed is anyone who will eat bread in the kingdom of God!"* [16]*Then Jesus said
to him, "Someone gave a great dinner and invited many.* [17]*At the time for the
dinner he sent his slave to say to those who had been invited, 'Come; for everything is ready now.'* [18]*But they all alike began to make excuses. The first said to
him, 'I have bought a piece of land, and I must go out and see it; please accept
my regrets.'* [19]*Another said, 'I have bought five yoke of oxen, and I am going to
try them out; please accept my regrets.'* [20]*Another said, 'I have just been married,
and therefore I cannot come.'* [21]*So the slave returned and reported this to his
master. Then the owner of the house became angry and said to his slave, 'Go out
at once into the streets and lanes of the town and bring in the poor, the crippled,
the blind, and the lame.'* [22]*And the slave said, 'Sir, what you ordered has been
done, and there is still room.'* [23]*Then the master said to the slave, 'Go out into
the roads and lanes, and compel people to come in, so that my house may be
filled.* [24]*For I tell you, none of those who were invited will taste my dinner.'"*

[25]*Now large crowds were traveling with him; and he turned and said to them,*
[26]*"Whoever comes to me and does not hate father and mother, wife and chil-*

37

dren, brothers and sisters, yes, and even life itself, cannot be my disciple.
²⁷Whoever does not carry the cross and follow me cannot be my disciple. ²⁸For
which of you, intending to build a tower, does not first sit down and estimate the
cost, to see whether he has enough to complete it? ²⁹Otherwise, when he has laid
a foundation and is not able to finish, all who see it will begin to ridicule him,
³⁰saying, 'This fellow began to build and was not able to finish.' ³¹Or what king,
going out to wage war against another king, will not sit down first and consider
whether he is able with ten thousand to oppose the one who comes against him
with twenty thousand? ³²If he cannot, then, while the other is still far away, he
sends a delegation and asks for the terms of peace. ³³So therefore, none of you
can become my disciple if you do not give up all your possessions."

While Jesus continues to dine at the house of a leading Pharisee, he continues to teach about God's kingdom using images of meals and banquets. Following his teachings on humility and generosity, one of the guests utters a beatitude: "Blessed is anyone who will eat bread in the kingdom of God!" Of course, most people sitting around Jesus at the feast assume that those who will eat at the banquet of God's kingdom are people much like themselves: religious leaders, scholars of the law, the wealthy and influential, and those in whose lives God's blessings seem most apparent. However, in his parable of the great banquet, Jesus suggests that those who will enter God's great meal are more like those not invited to other feasts.

As Jesus tells the parable, it seems that the invitations have already gone out to the expected crowd and those invited have responded with their commitment to attend. The master of the house sends out his servant to announce that everything is now ready and that the guests should come. But immediately those invited begin to make excuses. A variety of financial and familial concerns seems more important or urgent to them than attending the banquet. These excuses are insulting to the master of the house, and he is angered by this lack of courtesy. Rather than postponing the meal since it is ready, he acts quickly to change the plans. He sends his servant out into the city streets and back alleys of the town to invite the poor, disabled, and outcasts. The host desires that the banquet be given to a full house. When the servant reports that there is still room, the master sends him out to the highways outside the town, reaching out in all directions, encouraging everyone to attend.

The parable is a grand description of opportunity refused and divine grace bestowed. The religious leaders and others in line for God's blessings opt out of the invitation. The parable makes clear that this exclusion is not God's desire. Those invited reject the invitation and refuse to attend. But the abundant gift of the kingdom is not lost because some reject it. Many others are invited and will attend in multitudes. Some of those who were expected to be there will not enter, while many who were not originally expected will come in through God's gracious generosity. Jesus emphasizes that the time of God's kingdom is now and the response is urgent.

After the meal and as Jesus continues his journey, he begins to describe in more detail what discipleship requires. Essentially Jesus teaches that those who follow him must count the costs of discipleship and make discipleship their life's first priority. The choice to follow after Jesus cannot be made casually. One must first assess the risks, then fully pursue the task, and finally complete the goal.

Jesus must hold the disciple's allegiance over all else, including family. The call to "hate" family members and even one's own life must not be read literally but as a form of hyperbole (verse 26). As deeply as one might love a parent or sibling, a spouse or child, one must love Jesus even more. Likewise, Jesus' call to give up all of one's possessions is exaggerated rhetoric (verse 33), but material possessions can be a great hindrance to discipleship. Pursuing discipleship means being attached to Jesus, not to possessions. No earthly attachment, neither family nor possessions, can deter one's pursuit of God's kingdom. Jesus must be the focus, the passion, and the goal of all who seek him. Discipleship is a relationship with Jesus and a commitment to him. It means carrying the cross and following him (verse 27). Following Jesus means suffering with him, bearing the pain of persecution, and sharing the fate of rejection by the world.

The decision for discipleship requires that we first assess the costs. As when considering whether or not to build a watchtower or to go into battle, one must assess one's resources. One must not begin a building project until one knows that it can be completed. A king must not go into battle until he knows he has the forces to be victorious. Likewise with discipleship: Jesus says that one must assess whether one is ready to take on the personal commitment and sacrifice required to follow Jesus.

Reflection and discussion

• How does this parable demonstrate that people can only remain outside of God's kingdom by their own deliberate choice?

• What does the master's desire that his house be filled say about God's grace and his desire that all people be saved?

• Why should the decision to be a disciple of Jesus be entered into only with sober and prudent reflection?

Prayer

Loving Lord, you have offered me the gift of God's kingdom to be experienced now and completely in the future. Help me to assess the costs of being your disciple, and give me the grace to focus my life on you.

"I tell you, there will be more joy in heaven over one sinner who repents than over ninety-nine righteous persons who need no repentance." Luke 15:7

Searching, Finding, and Rejoicing

LUKE 15:1–10 ¹*Now all the tax collectors and sinners were coming near to listen to him. ²And the Pharisees and the scribes were grumbling and saying, "This fellow welcomes sinners and eats with them."*

³So he told them this parable: ⁴"Which one of you, having a hundred sheep and losing one of them, does not leave the ninety-nine in the wilderness and go after the one that is lost until he finds it? ⁵When he has found it, he lays it on his shoulders and rejoices. ⁶And when he comes home, he calls together his friends and neighbors, saying to them, 'Rejoice with me, for I have found my sheep that was lost.' ⁷Just so, I tell you, there will be more joy in heaven over one sinner who repents than over ninety-nine righteous persons who need no repentance.

⁸"Or what woman having ten silver coins, if she loses one of them, does not light a lamp, sweep the house, and search carefully until she finds it? ⁹When she has found it, she calls together her friends and neighbors, saying, 'Rejoice with me, for I have found the coin that I had lost.' ¹⁰Just so, I tell you, there is joy in the presence of the angels of God over one sinner who repents."

J esus never excludes anyone from his presence, but he has a special affection for the poor and outcasts. His affection for the outsiders is reciprocated, and Luke introduces this section of the gospel by noting that "all the tax collectors and sinners were coming near to listen to him." They are attracted to him because he welcomes them and is willing to eat with them. Some religious leaders criticize Jesus for his choice of company, and they disparagingly identify him as the one who "welcomes sinners and eats with them." In these parables Jesus explains why he welcomes and cares for sinners.

The first parable tells of a shepherd who is trying to account for all his sheep and discovers that one is missing. The shepherd leaves the rest of his flock and gives his undivided attention to seeking the lost one. His search continues until he locates the animal, places it on his shoulders, and brings it home rejoicing. Considering that the sheep could have been stolen or destroyed by wild animals, the shepherd calls his friends and neighbors together to celebrate his find.

Jesus' application points out that the parable describes the heart of God for sinners. There is great rejoicing in heaven over the repentance of one sinner. In fact, God expresses greater joy over one repentant sinner than over ninety-nine righteous people. The possibility of finding the lost is the reason why Jesus "welcomes sinners and eats with them." He urges disciples to share in his passionate desire to seek the lost.

The second parable tells of a woman who discovers that one of her silver coins is lost. Although the drachma represents only a modest amount of money, the woman proceeds on a thorough search. She lights a lamp to help her see and sweeps the house with a broom, hoping to brush it out of some corner or hear its sound on the floor. She searches diligently until she finds the lost one. Then she calls her female friends and neighbors to celebrate the find with her.

The two parables are almost exactly parallel. They both describe a relentless search for what is lost and express irresistible joy at the find. God is like the shepherd and the woman. The point of each story is that God will go to great efforts and rejoice with great joy to find and restore a sinner to himself. In a culture where tax collectors are despised and sinners are shunned, Jesus offers teachings that encourage the rejected to come to him. His response to wayward people is strongly contrasted with that of the grumbling religious leaders. Jesus is the model for his disciples. Their mission, like that of Jesus, is to love people and draw them to God. They must reflect his concern and compassion, seeking out the lost and rejoicing with the heavens over every repentant sinner.

Reflection and discussion

• Why does Jesus tell these parables in response to the religious leaders' grumbling about Jesus welcoming sinners and eating with them?

• In what ways do the compassionate shepherd and the determined woman represent God?

• How do these two parables make you feel about your value to God?

Prayer

Lord Jesus, thank you for searching for me and finding me. Give me a heart for the lost of our world, and help me to rejoice with you over every repentant person who enters your embrace.

"This son of mine was dead and is alive again; he was lost and is found!" And they began to celebrate. Luke 15:24

Parable of the Forgiving Father

LUKE 15:11–32 ¹¹*Then Jesus said, "There was a man who had two sons.* ¹²*The younger of them said to his father, 'Father, give me the share of the property that will belong to me.' So he divided his property between them.* ¹³*A few days later the younger son gathered all he had and traveled to a distant country, and there he squandered his property in dissolute living.* ¹⁴*When he had spent everything, a severe famine took place throughout that country, and he began to be in need.* ¹⁵*So he went and hired himself out to one of the citizens of that country, who sent him to his fields to feed the pigs.* ¹⁶*He would gladly have filled himself with the pods that the pigs were eating; and no one gave him anything.* ¹⁷*But when he came to himself he said, 'How many of my father's hired hands have bread enough and to spare, but here I am dying of hunger!* ¹⁸*I will get up and go to my father, and I will say to him, "Father, I have sinned against heaven and before you;* ¹⁹*I am no longer worthy to be called your son; treat me like one of your hired hands."'* ²⁰*So he set off and went to his father. But while he was still far off, his father saw him and was filled with compassion; he ran and put his arms around him and kissed him.* ²¹*Then the son said to him, 'Father, I have sinned against heaven and before you; I am no longer worthy to be called your son.'* ²²*But the father said to his slaves, 'Quickly, bring out a robe—the best one—*

and put it on him; put a ring on his finger and sandals on his feet. ²³*And get the fatted calf and kill it, and let us eat and celebrate;* ²⁴*for this son of mine was dead and is alive again; he was lost and is found!' And they began to celebrate.*

²⁵*"Now his elder son was in the field; and when he came and approached the house, he heard music and dancing.* ²⁶*He called one of the slaves and asked what was going on.* ²⁷*He replied, 'Your brother has come, and your father has killed the fatted calf, because he has got him back safe and sound.'* ²⁸*Then he became angry and refused to go in. His father came out and began to plead with him.* ²⁹*But he answered his father, 'Listen! For all these years I have been working like a slave for you, and I have never disobeyed your command; yet you have never given me even a young goat so that I might celebrate with my friends.* ³⁰*But when this son of yours came back, who has devoured your property with prostitutes, you killed the fatted calf for him!'* ³¹*Then the father said to him, 'Son, you are always with me, and all that is mine is yours.* ³²*But we had to celebrate and rejoice, because this brother of yours was dead and has come to life; he was lost and has been found.'"*

T he parable of the lost son and the forgiving father is the third parable to demonstrate God's love for wayward sinners and his compassionate desire for their repentance. In the context of Jesus' dialogue with the religious leaders and his instruction to sinners who have come to hear him, the prodigal son is an image of sinners, the older son is an image of the religious leaders, and the father is an image of God. The focus of the parable is the father's reaction to each of the two sons.

At the request of the younger son, the father divides all his property between his two sons. The father expresses the unfathomable grace of God, and the two sons embody two different attitudes that prevent people from experiencing God's abundance. The younger son is lost in his wasteful lifestyle, and the older son is lost in his self-righteousness.

The younger son squanders his inheritance, is reduced to famine, and longs to eat the food of the pigs. Coming to his senses, he prepares a script to deliver to his father, hoping to be accepted back as a hired hand. The son makes the first move, turning around and moving toward the father. That's all he needs to do. The father, who has been watching and waiting for him all along, spots him a long way off. He runs to his son, embraces him, and kisses him. The emotion of the joyous father creates a scene of overwhelming love and for-giveness. Though the son identifies himself with the stigma of his sins, the father is bent on helping him reverse his shame-filled mindset. The fine robe, the ring, the sandals, and the feast of veal all proclaim the lost sinner as the father's true and beloved child.

The older son has been "in the field." He is the worker, the one who is responsible and has always done everything his father asked of him. When he hears the music and dancing and realizes his father is celebrating the return of the younger son, he becomes angry and refuses to enter the house. But the father who ran toward one lost son now comes after the other son. The older son complains, "For all these years I have been working like a slave for you, and I have never disobeyed your command." He is lost in his self-pity and bit-ter resentment, and he is unable to live the joyful life of a beloved child of his father.

Although sinners are mirrored in the attitude of the younger son and the religious leaders are mirrored in the mindset of the older son, the parable is addressed to all of Luke's readers. We are all lost children who have been found by our Father. Yet we maintain ways of thinking about God that deprive us of joy in our Father's presence. Either we remain identified with our past sins and cannot accept the fact that we are really sons and daughters, or we follow orders with obedience and can't believe that the Father's love is unmer-ited and free. Only when we accept our Father's unlimited grace with joy and gratitude can we truly celebrate and feel at home with God.

Reflection and discussion

• When have I seen God's forgiveness enable a person to leave behind a mis-guided past and begin a life transformed by hope and confidence?

• What do I see of myself in the mindset of each of the two sons?

• What most prevents me from experiencing the abundant love of God?

• How do the parables of the lost sheep, the lost coin, and the lost son challenge and transform my understanding of God?

Prayer

Father of compassionate mercy, I have wandered from your care and have become lost in selfishness. I desire to turn back to you with all my heart so that I can experience the joy of being at home with you.

"If then you have not been faithful with the dishonest wealth, who will entrust to you the true riches? And if you have not been faithful with what belongs to another, who will give you what is your own?" Luke 16:11–12

Handling Money and Possessions Generously

LUKE 16:1–13 ¹*Then Jesus said to the disciples, "There was a rich man who had a manager, and charges were brought to him that this man was squandering his property. ²So he summoned him and said to him, 'What is this that I hear about you? Give me an accounting of your management, because you cannot be my manager any longer.' ³Then the manager said to himself, 'What will I do, now that my master is taking the position away from me? I am not strong enough to dig, and I am ashamed to beg. ⁴I have decided what to do so that, when I am dismissed as manager, people may welcome me into their homes.' ⁵So, summoning his master's debtors one by one, he asked the first, 'How much do you owe my master?' ⁶He answered, 'A hundred jugs of olive oil.' He said to him, 'Take your bill, sit down quickly, and make it fifty.' ⁷Then he asked another, 'And how much do you owe?' He replied, 'A hundred containers of wheat.' He said to him, 'Take your bill and make it eighty.' ⁸And his master commended the dishonest manager because he had acted shrewdly; for the children of this age are more shrewd in dealing with their own generation than are the children of light. ⁹And I tell you, make friends for yourselves by means of dishonest wealth so that when it is gone, they may welcome you into the eternal homes.*

^{10} "Whoever is faithful in a very little is faithful also in much; and whoever is dishonest in a very little is dishonest also in much. ^{11} If then you have not been faithful with the dishonest wealth, who will entrust to you the true riches? ^{12} And if you have not been faithful with what belongs to another, who will give you what is your own? ^{13} No slave can serve two masters; for a slave will either hate the one and love the other, or be devoted to the one and despise the other. You cannot serve God and wealth."

Through the use of parables, Jesus continues to teach his disciples the ways of God's kingdom. Although this parable of the shrewd manager seems simple enough in its details, its interpretation is particularly difficult, largely because of the wealthy man's praise of his manager at the end of the parable for what seems to be dishonest deals (verse 8). Why does Jesus hold this manager up as an example for his disciples to imitate? A deeper understanding of the parable helps us consider its interpretation and application to discipleship.

Those who managed the estates of wealthy landowners made a living by collecting debts and rents for their masters and charging the debtors commissions which would go into the managers' own coffers. The manager in this parable has been dismissed by his rich master, so he is trying to decide how he will ensure a secure future for himself. Knowing that his job is gone and unable to do manual labor, he needs to devise a solution that will leave him able to find work from sympathetic business associates. He settles on a plan to reduce the debt of each debtor by cancelling his own commission. This will undoubtedly make some grateful constituents who will be willing to either hire him or welcome him into their homes in the future. He is not trying to hide anything from his wealthy master; the master is still owed what is due to him. However, the former manager, by foregoing some of his own commissions, creates a brighter future for himself. Although we don't know the details of how the manager squandered his master's property or why the master dismissed him, we do know that the master commends him for the shrewd way he acts to secure his own future.

Jesus highlights the point that the shrewd manager used the means at his disposal to guarantee his future. He remarks that people who focus on this world ("the children of this age") give more foresight to their future than do the people of God ("the children of light"). Jesus is saying that disciples should be as thorough in assessing the long-term future of their actions as worldly people are in protecting their well-being. They should apply themselves to honor and serve God with their possessions as much as worldly people apply themselves to obtain security from money and favor.

Jesus continues to draw lessons from the parable for his disciples. First, he says that they should not hoard their wealth or use it selfishly; rather, they should use it to make friends for themselves (verse 9). In other words, Jesus urges his disciples to use their money generously because it doesn't last beyond death. By using their money to help the poor and for other good works, disciples make friends who will welcome them into their eternal home. Second, Jesus teaches that the way a person makes use of "very little" is evidence of how that person will make use of "much" (verse 10). All of one's activities reveal the nature of one's character. If followers of Jesus cannot handle worldly wealth with generosity, then they cannot be entrusted with wealth that lasts forever (verse 11). Finally, Jesus states, "You cannot serve God and wealth" (verse 13). Disciples must use their wealth for God's purposes, but they must not become enslaved to it. Those who follow Jesus owe their total allegiance to God alone.

Reflection and discussion

• What is one lesson Jesus wants me to understand from the parable of the shrewd manager?

• What kind of long-term investment does this parable invite me to make?

• How does Jesus desire me to use temporary wealth to obtain everlasting wealth?

• Why does Jesus address verses 10-12 to all present and future disciples? In what way do these verses speak to disciples today?

• Why can a follower of Jesus not serve both God and wealth? What happens when I try to serve both God and wealth?

Prayer

Lord God, all that I have—my money, my possessions, my talents, my time—is on loan from you. Show me how to use wisely what you have entrusted to me. Give me the foresight of the shrewd manager in preparing for my eternal future.

"Child, remember that during your lifetime you received your good things, and Lazarus in like manner evil things; but now he is comforted here, and you are in agony." Luke 16:25

Parable of the Rich Man and Lazarus

LUKE 16:19–31 [19]*"There was a rich man who was dressed in purple and fine linen and who feasted sumptuously every day.* [20]*And at his gate lay a poor man named Lazarus, covered with sores,* [21]*who longed to satisfy his hunger with what fell from the rich man's table; even the dogs would come and lick his sores.* [22]*The poor man died and was carried away by the angels to be with Abraham. The rich man also died and was buried.* [23]*In Hades, where he was being tormented, he looked up and saw Abraham far away with Lazarus by his side.* [24]*He called out, 'Father Abraham, have mercy on me, and send Lazarus to dip the tip of his finger in water and cool my tongue; for I am in agony in these flames.'* [25]*But Abraham said, 'Child, remember that during your lifetime you received your good things, and Lazarus in like manner evil things; but now he is comforted here, and you are in agony.* [26]*Besides all this, between you and us a great chasm has been fixed, so that those who might want to pass from here to you cannot do so, and no one can cross from there to us.'* [27]*He said, 'Then, father, I beg you to send him to my father's house—*[28]*for I have five brothers—that he may warn them, so that they will not also come into this place of torment.'* [29]*Abraham replied, 'They have Moses and the prophets; they should listen to* *them.' ³⁰He said, 'No, father Abraham; but if someone goes to them from the dead, they will repent.' ³¹He said to him, 'If they do not listen to Moses and the prophets, neither will they be convinced even if someone rises from the dead.'"*

Jesus tells a second parable about wealth and possessions. The situations of the rich man and Lazarus could not be more starkly contrasted. The rich man dressed in the finest clothing and feasted sumptuously, not just on special occasions but "every day." The poor man was covered with ulcerated sores and lay among the dogs. Starving, he longed to eat the scraps that fell from the table of the rich man. Lazarus lay at the gate of the rich man's home, so evidently the rich man passed him by each day without notice or concern.

Both men died: the poor man obviously from starvation and disease, the rich man probably from conditions that afflict those who feast habitually on rich foods and strong drink. But in the next life their conditions are dramatically reversed. The rich man ends up in torment, and the poor man resides at the side of Abraham. The one who failed to show mercy in his earthly life now begs for mercy from Abraham. Not only are their roles reversed, but they are intensified. Abraham's reply sums up the dramatic turnaround: the one who received good things during his lifetime is in "agony" in the afterlife, while the one who received evil things on earth is "comforted" in Abraham's embrace (verse 25). The rich man's agony far exceeds the misery poor Lazarus ever experienced in earthly life, while the bliss of Lazarus far exceeds the pleasure the rich man had ever known.

Although the rich man seemed not to notice Lazarus on earth, he now appeals through Abraham for the poor man's aid. The rich man requests that Lazarus put just a drop of water on his parched tongue to relieve his anguish. The request is a small one, but it recalls Lazarus' similarly small request for scraps of food. Just as there were no crumbs for Lazarus, there will be no water for the rich man. He has sealed his own fate. The rich man is not condemned because he is rich, but because he showed a callous disregard for the needs of others that wealth often produces. He became consumed with his own pleasures and lifestyle and failed to respond to the suffering and needs of others around him. His callousness made his earthly riches all he would ever receive from life.

The rich man's neglect of the poor man at his gate is a clear rejection of "Moses and the prophets" (verse 29). The law of Moses demands, "If there is among you anyone in need…do not be hard-hearted or tight-fisted toward your needy neighbor" (Deut 15:7). Likewise, the prophets do not relent: "Share your bread with the hungry, and bring the homeless poor into your house" (Isa 58:7). When the rich man asked that Lazarus be sent to warn his five brothers to repent, Abraham declared, finally, that if the rich man's brothers do not listen to the clear words of Scripture given by Moses and the prophets, they will also reject the message of Jesus, even when he is risen from the dead (verse 31).

The word of God, discovered in Scripture and the teachings of Jesus, is capable of generating repentance only in a receptive heart. To reject the message of Moses and the prophets is to reject the teachings of Jesus. The heart cannot see what it is not looking for. Those with responsive hearts will listen to God's message, come to receive his forgiveness, experience the faith that leads to understanding, and experience compassion for those in need.

Reflection and discussion

• Which words of this parable have the most impact on me? What parts of the parable make me uncomfortable?

• In what ways does the parable continue the theme of reversal that we've seen throughout Luke's gospel?

• Jesus addresses this parable to the Pharisees, in whose theology God and wealth are comfortably joined. How would Jesus respond to the so-called prosperity gospel often preached today?

• As examples of the teachings of "Moses and the prophets," read Deuteronomy 15:7-11 and Isaiah 58:6-7. How do these Scriptures demonstrate that the rich man violates the Torah and prophets?

• Since the rich man and his five brothers have the clear teachings of the Scriptures, what is their problem? When do I have similar problems in grasping the meaning of Scripture?

Prayer

Lord of the living and the dead, help me to raise my eyes from my own needs so that I can see the needs of others. Give me a receptive heart to listen to your word in Scripture and a responsive heart to live my life in a way that gives glory to you.

SUGGESTIONS FOR FACILITATORS, GROUP SESSION 3

1. Welcome group members and ask if there are any announcements anyone would like to make.

2. You may want to pray this prayer as a group:

> God of Abraham, Moses, and the prophets, you have sent your Son as the completion of your revelation to the world. As we read Luke's gospel, we are privileged to sit at table with Jesus and travel with him along the way to Jerusalem, all the while learning from him to be disciples. Detach us from the lure of material wealth, temporal securities, and worldly influence in order to open our hearts to receive your grace. Give us humility, trust, and generosity so that we may receive the gift of your kingdom with responsive hearts and live always in a way that gives glory to you.

3. Ask one or more of the following questions:
   - Which image from lessons 7–12 stands out most memorably to you?
   - What is the most important thing you learned through your study this week?

4. Discuss lessons 7 through 12. Choose one or more of the questions for reflection and discussion from each lesson to discuss as a group. You may want to ask group members which question was most challenging or helpful to them as you review each lesson.

5. Remember that there are no definitive answers for these discussion questions. The insights of group members will add to the understanding of all. None of these questions require an expert.

6. After talking about each lesson, instruct group members to complete lessons 13 through 18 on their own during the six days before the next group meeting. They should write out their own answers to the questions as preparation for next week's group discussion.

7. Ask the group if anyone is having any particular problems with the Bible study during the week. You may want to share advice and encouragement within the group.

8. Conclude by praying aloud together the prayer at the end of one of the lessons discussed. You may add to the prayer based on the sharing that has occurred in the group.

"When you have done all that you were ordered to do, say, 'We are worthless slaves; we have done only what we ought to have done!'" Luke 17:10

The Faith to Do What Jesus Requires

LUKE 17:1–10 ¹*Jesus said to his disciples, "Occasions for stumbling are bound to come, but woe to anyone by whom they come! ²It would be better for you if a millstone were hung around your neck and you were thrown into the sea than for you to cause one of these little ones to stumble. ³Be on your guard! If another disciple sins, you must rebuke the offender, and if there is repentance, you must forgive. ⁴And if the same person sins against you seven times a day, and turns back to you seven times and says, 'I repent,' you must forgive."*

⁵*The apostles said to the Lord, "Increase our faith!" ⁶The Lord replied, "If you had faith the size of a mustard seed, you could say to this mulberry tree, 'Be uprooted and planted in the sea,' and it would obey you.*

⁷*"Who among you would say to your slave who has just come in from plowing or tending sheep in the field, 'Come here at once and take your place at the table'? ⁸Would you not rather say to him, 'Prepare supper for me, put on your apron and serve me while I eat and drink; later you may eat and drink'? ⁹Do you thank the slave for doing what was commanded? ¹⁰So you also, when you have done all that you were ordered to do, say, 'We are worthless slaves; we have done only what we ought to have done!'"*

Jesus speaks about four characteristics of discipleship as he travels with them along the way. He teaches his followers to avoid causing scandal (verses 1–2), to forgive the repentant believer (verses 3–4), to exercise faith (verses 5–6), and to maintain a servant's attitude (verses 7–10). Though these seem to be a collection of teachings with different themes, Luke has gathered them under the broad category of faithfulness.

Jesus tells his disciples that occasions for "stumbling" are bound to present themselves among his disciples. The Greek work is *skandalon,* meaning anything that causes one to trip and fall. Such occasions that could cause believers to lose faith or to entice them to sin must be avoided at all costs within the community of faith. Jesus issues another prophetic "woe" to anyone causing such scandal within the community of faith. With a graphic image, Jesus describes the seriousness of causing "one of these little ones" to fall. The millstone is the heavy stone of a grinding mill. Needless to say, when hung around the neck, it would make drowning certain. The "little ones" are new disciples who are still in need of instructions or disciples whose faith is weak. With this saying, Jesus emphasizes the importance of teaching disciples within the community and guiding them to maturity in the faith.

Disciples have a responsibility to reprimand one another about sin and to forgive one another upon repentance. This means that disciples are accountable to one another and share in each other's commitment to deepen their relationship with Jesus. Faith is not a private affair. As brothers and sisters of one another, disciples must rebuke sin and forgive one another as a familial responsibility. The ability to forgive allows people to move past their failures. So each time the request for forgiveness is made, when repentance is genuine, it must be granted. Just as God's forgiveness is without limit, so must be that of the disciple.

When the apostles ask Jesus to help them increase their faith, they are expressing their understanding that faith is not a moment, but a journey. They recognize their need for guidance and direction from Jesus as they grow in faith. Those with maturing faith will be less likely to stumble, and they will not waver in the face of opposition. Jesus does not directly respond to their request because he knows that their faith will certainly grow through further teaching, example, and the sending of the Spirit. Rather, he responds by assuring them that even a little faith is capable of amazing things. Of course, the image of the tree being replanted in the sea is another example of hyperbolic

language, which is not to be understood literally. Rather, the illustration pro-
vokes wonder in the disciples about the capacity of their own faith. They
already have sufficient faith to live by the teachings Jesus has just given them,
even if it may seem impossible.

The fourth characteristic of discipleship taught by Jesus is maintaining the
outlook of a servant. He illustrates this attitude by describing the end of the
day for slaves who have been plowing a field or tending sheep. The master
does not sit them down and serve them a meal out of gratitude. No, the slaves
continue to serve out of a sense of duty and consider themselves to be their
master's unworthy servants. Just so, disciples are God's servants, working
faithfully and dutifully. They should not expect praise and reward for performing the tasks that they are obligated to perform. The proper attitude of
disciples is thankfulness for having the privilege and opportunity to serve
God. Whatever reward we have for serving God is not merited, but is given
because God is gracious.

Reflection and discussion

• Who are the "little ones" in the church today who can easily trip and fall?
What is my responsibility toward them?

• Why are repentance and forgiveness so critical in the Christian community?
How can I continually forgive without reinforcing bad behavior?

• What is the truth contained in Jesus' saying in verse 6? How does it provoke wonder in me?

• What does it mean to have a servant's mindset as a disciple? How can I be a better servant?

•Which of these four characteristics of faithful discipleship gives me the most difficulty? How might dealing with this quality affect the other three qualities?

Prayer

Jesus, Master, you have given me the gift and privilege of being your disciple. Keep me on guard so that I will not cause others to stumble, and increase my faith so that I will be able to trust you and forgive others.

"In fact, the kingdom of God is among you." Luke 17:21

The Presence and the Coming of the Kingdom

LUKE 17:11–37   ¹¹*On the way to Jerusalem Jesus was going through the region between Samaria and Galilee. *¹²*As he entered a village, ten lepers approached him. Keeping their distance, *¹³*they called out, saying, "Jesus, Master, have mercy on us!" *¹⁴*When he saw them, he said to them, "Go and show yourselves to the priests." And as they went, they were made clean. *¹⁵*Then one of them, when he saw that he was healed, turned back, praising God with a loud voice. *¹⁶*He prostrated himself at Jesus' feet and thanked him. And he was a Samaritan. *¹⁷*Then Jesus asked, "Were not ten made clean? But the other nine, where are they? *¹⁸*Was none of them found to return and give praise to God except this foreigner?" *¹⁹*Then he said to him, "Get up and go on your way; your faith has made you well."*

²⁰*Once Jesus was asked by the Pharisees when the kingdom of God was coming, and he answered, "The kingdom of God is not coming with things that can be observed; *²¹*nor will they say, 'Look, here it is!' or 'There it is!' For, in fact, the kingdom of God is among you."*

²²Then he said to the disciples, "The days are coming when you will long to see one of the days of the Son of Man, and you will not see it. ²³They will say to you, 'Look there!' or 'Look here!' Do not go, do not set off in pursuit. ²⁴For as the lightning flashes and lights up the sky from one side to the other, so will the Son of Man be in his day. ²⁵But first he must endure much suffering and be rejected by this generation. ²⁶Just as it was in the days of Noah, so too it will be in the days of the Son of Man. ²⁷They were eating and drinking, and marrying and being given in marriage, until the day Noah entered the ark, and the flood came and destroyed all of them. ²⁸Likewise, just as it was in the days of Lot: they were eating and drinking, buying and selling, planting and building, ²⁹but on the day that Lot left Sodom, it rained fire and sulfur from heaven and destroyed all of them—³⁰it will be like that on the day that the Son of Man is revealed. ³¹On that day, anyone on the housetop who has belongings in the house must not come down to take them away; and likewise anyone in the field must not turn back. ³²Remember Lot's wife. ³³Those who try to make their life secure will lose it, but those who lose their life will keep it. ³⁴I tell you, on that night there will be two in one bed; one will be taken and the other left. ³⁵There will be two women grinding meal together; one will be taken and the other left." ³⁷Then they asked him, "Where, Lord?" He said to them, "Where the corpse is, there the vultures will gather."

While Jesus continues to travel "on the way to Jerusalem," ten lepers call out to him. Unable to get near because of their contagion, they beg for his mercy. Jesus directs them to go to the priests, who would certify their healing and allow them to return to society. As they were on their way, "they were made clean." The encounter then focuses on "one of them," the only one who turns back after realizing he has been healed. He gives praise to God and prostrates himself at Jesus' feet in gratitude. His closeness to Jesus contrasts with the distance he observed when asking Jesus for mercy. The account further highlights this man's uniqueness by noting that he is a Samaritan, an outsider who is shunned by Jews as much as lepers.

Jesus then asks three rhetorical questions, emphasizing the absence of the other nine healed lepers in contrast to "this foreigner" (verses 17–18). He is really making a stinging observation about the nine who have missed their opportunity. The Samaritan alone demonstrates the faith that saves. Although all ten were healed by Jesus, only one responds in a personal way and enters a relationship to Jesus. Once again in Luke's gospel, a Samaritan is the model of faith and genuine response to God's grace.

The reaction of the Samaritan leads to a discussion about the kingdom of God. Jesus tries to correct the Pharisees' perception that the kingdom is tied to specific future events to which they can point by looking here or there (verses 20–21). Like many Jews of the time, the Pharisees thought that the arrival of God's kingdom would be so clear and powerful that magnificent signs from heaven would announce it. Jesus explains, "In fact, the kingdom of God is among you." They must understand that the kingdom has already come, at least in its initial manifestation, in Jesus himself. All who respond to him with faith, like the grateful Samaritan, experience the kingdom within themselves and among the community of fellow believers.

While the kingdom of God has come in Jesus, it will achieve its glorious completion in the future. To experience God's plan for his kingdom, both now and in the future, one must look to Jesus and the salvation he offers. He is the glorious Son of Man who will be revealed on that day. When he appears, he will come as quickly and as visibly as lightning lights up the sky (verse 24). There will be judgment and destruction as swift and permanent as that which occurred in the days of Noah and Lot (verses 26–30). As in those days, when injustice and oppression were judged with destruction, the righteous like Noah and Lot will be saved. Those who look back and try to preserve their life, like the wife of Lot, will lose their life, but those who are willing to lose their life, making no permanent claims to it, will preserve it forever (verses 32–33). When the Son of Man appears, there will be division between people. Some will be judged ready to be taken into God's kingdom; others will be left outside (verses 34–35).

The apocalyptic and sometimes cryptic language of these verses is rich in symbolism and must not be understood as literal illustrations of the final coming. As a prophetic warning, its purpose is to highlight the critical importance of responding to the grace of God manifested in Jesus and to encourage repentance. Although the coming of the Son of Man may not be seen for a long time, disciples must not grow complacent; rather, they must be vigilant, waiting always with expectation.

Reflection and discussion

• What is the point Luke is making by emphasizing that the one healed leper who returned to praise God and thank Jesus was a Samaritan?

• In what sense is the kingdom of God present among us? In what sense is God's kingdom to be expected in the future?

• What is the meaning of Jesus' warning, "Those who try to make their life secure will lose it"? What is the meaning of his promise, "Those who lose their life will keep it"?

Prayer

Jesus, Master, have mercy and heal me. As you continue to make me whole, help me to recognize that the kingdom of God is among us. May I always give you thanks as I await the fullness of the kingdom when you will come in glory.

"The tax collector, standing far off, would not even look up to heaven, but was beating his breast and saying, 'God, be merciful to me, a sinner!'"

Luke 18:13

Parables on Persistent and Humble Prayer

LUKE 18:1–14 ¹*Then Jesus told them a parable about their need to pray always and not to lose heart.* ²*He said, "In a certain city there was a judge who neither feared God nor had respect for people.* ³*In that city there was a widow who kept coming to him and saying, 'Grant me justice against my opponent.'* ⁴*For a while he refused; but later he said to himself, 'Though I have no fear of God and no respect for anyone,* ⁵*yet because this widow keeps bothering me, I will grant her justice, so that she may not wear me out by continually coming.'"* ⁶*And the Lord said, "Listen to what the unjust judge says.* ⁷*And will not God grant justice to his chosen ones who cry to him day and night? Will he delay long in helping them?* ⁸*I tell you, he will quickly grant justice to them. And yet, when the Son of Man comes, will he find faith on earth?"*

⁹*He also told this parable to some who trusted in themselves that they were righteous and regarded others with contempt:* ¹⁰*"Two men went up to the temple to pray, one a Pharisee and the other a tax collector.* ¹¹*The Pharisee, standing by himself, was praying thus, 'God, I thank you that I am not like other people: thieves, rogues, adulterers, or even like this tax collector.* ¹²*I fast twice a week; I give a tenth of all my income.'* ¹³*But the tax collector, standing far off, would not*

even look up to heaven, but was beating his breast and saying, 'God, be merciful to me, a sinner!' [14]*I tell you, this man went down to his home justified rather than the other; for all who exalt themselves will be humbled, but all who humble themselves will be exalted."*

Each of these two parables portrays two central characters: the first shows us the widow and the judge; the second shows us the Pharisee and the tax collector. Each story opens with a statement of purpose (vv. 1, 9) and concludes with summary comments (vv. 6–8, 14). As parables, they each challenge the inner disposition of the hearers—both the disciples of Jesus' day and those in succeeding generations who hear the gospel proclaimed. Prayer, they teach us, is not just a matter of right words or proper technique. Rather, it concerns our relationship with God and our changed hearts.

Widows, like orphans and aliens, were defenseless and had no social standing. Yet, this widow eventually receives justice from the judge, not because she is powerful or because the judge is compassionate, but because she is relentless in her pursuit of justice. She will not take no for an answer and she wears him down. The point of the parable is clear. If this defenseless widow can achieve justice from a heartless judge through persistence, how much more can we expect that God, the just and merciful judge, will answer our prayers if we persevere.

The introduction states that the parable is about the need "to pray always and not to lose heart." This means that prayer is not about the quantity of words we say, but about our whole relationship with God. Praying always means making our whole life a response to God. The conclusion asks whether or not the Son of Man will find faith on earth when he comes again (verse 8). This implies that persistent prayer is necessary to maintain a living faith while we wait for the fullness of God's kingdom. Faith prompts us to pray, and prayer strengthens our faith. Disciples must continue to pray with vigilance and not lose heart in order to be found faithful when the Lord returns.

The second parable contrasts the prayer of the Pharisee and the tax collector. If we remember that the Pharisees at the time of Jesus were seen as the models of religious learning and devotion while tax collectors were despised as corrupt collaborators with the Roman occupiers, we can better comprehend the impact of Jesus' story. When these two men went up to the temple to pray, the differences in their internal dispositions are obvious. The Pharisee depends on his adherence to all the laws of his faith, and he assumes that he is righteous before God (verses 11–12). He thanks God that he is not like the tax collector standing nearby. The Pharisee exalts himself by listing all that he does for God and has no real sense of his own sinfulness and unworthiness before God. In contrast, the tax collector humbles himself, confesses that he is a sinner, and cries out for God's mercy (verse 13). He makes no comparison with others, and he knows that the only way to improve his relationship with God is to rely on his merciful grace. Jesus concludes the parable by stating that the tax collector, not the Pharisee, went home justified before God. What the Pharisee strove to achieve through his own efforts, the tax collector received as God's gift.

Jesus teaches that people can never earn or deserve salvation. The grace of God's forgiveness and the gift of justification before God mean that no one can feel religiously superior to another. The parable's conclusion warns disciples not to exalt themselves before God lest they be humbled. Again, Jesus shows how God honors humility and reverses human expectations. Prayer should be unassuming and honest, not trying to convince God of our righteousness but acknowledging our dependence on his grace and mercy.

Reflection and discussion

• How does the first parable challenge the discouragement I sometimes experience in prayer and urge me to pray always?

• If Jesus told the second parable today in order to communicate the same point, what group of people would be the Pharisee and who would be the tax collector?

• Why did the Pharisee act the way he did? Why did the tax collector act the way he did? What do I see of myself in each character?

• How do these two parables complement each other? What do they both teach me about prayer?

Prayer

Compassionate God, you are the just and merciful judge who hears and answers my prayers. I come before you, grateful for your gift of forgiveness and salvation, and confidently trusting in your grace.

When Jesus came to the place, he looked up and said to him, "Zacchaeus, hurry and come down; for I must stay at your house today." So he hurried down and was happy to welcome him. Luke 19:5–6

Jesus Reaches Out to Save the Lost

LUKE 19:1–10 ¹*He entered Jericho and was passing through it. ²A man was there named Zacchaeus; he was a chief tax collector and was rich. ³He was trying to see who Jesus was, but on account of the crowd he could not, because he was short in stature. ⁴So he ran ahead and climbed a sycamore tree to see him, because he was going to pass that way. ⁵When Jesus came to the place, he looked up and said to him, "Zacchaeus, hurry and come down; for I must stay at your house today." ⁶So he hurried down and was happy to welcome him. ⁷All who saw it began to grumble and said, "He has gone to be the guest of one who is a sinner." ⁸Zacchaeus stood there and said to the Lord, "Look, half of my possessions, Lord, I will give to the poor; and if I have defrauded anyone of anything, I will pay back four times as much." ⁹Then Jesus said to him, "Today salvation has come to this house, because he too is a son of Abraham. ¹⁰For the Son of Man came to seek out and to save the lost."*

Jesus enters the city of Jericho, indicating that his journey to Jerusalem is nearing its goal. Jericho is in the Jordan River valley, just north of the Dead Sea, and served as a tax collection center. At Jericho travelers turned west and began the uphill journey to Jerusalem. Jericho is 850 feet below sea level, and Jerusalem is 2500 feet above sea level. Since the feast of Passover was drawing near, crowds of pilgrims on their way to Jerusalem would be passing through Jericho.

As a chief tax collector for the region, Zacchaeus would have been well-known in the town. He bid for the contract from Roman authorities, organized the collection, and took a cut from the labor of the tax collectors who worked for him. It is no surprise, then, that the account describes him as a wealthy man. He is most likely Jewish and has heard reports about Jesus, and now he has an opportunity to see Jesus for himself. Yet, Zacchaeus encounters two obstacles: first, the crowd is so large that he cannot get a look at Jesus, and second, he is short in stature and cannot see above the crowd. Clearly Zacchaeus is more than idly curious about Jesus. For in order to see Jesus, he runs ahead of the crowd and climbs a sycamore tree to get a good vantage point. Such action, like running through the crowd and climbing a tree, were unbecoming of a man of wealth and influence. His undignified action probably evoked scorn, derision, and laughter from the townspeople. Yet, Zacchaeus is determined to get a look at Jesus. He seems to be very attracted to him, yet reluctant to approach him personally.

When Jesus arrives under the tree in which Zacchaeus is perched, Jesus looks up and addresses him by name: "Zacchaeus, hurry and come down; for I must stay at your house today." Although Jesus was planning to pass through Jericho, not intending to stop there on his way to Jerusalem, he changes his plans upon seeing Zacchaeus in the tree. There is a sense of urgent necessity in Jesus' words. His occupation, sinfulness, dishonesty, and greed were no barrier to the heart of Jesus. He takes the initiative to enter into the life of the tax collector.

Zacchaeus, who was only hoping for a good view of Jesus, will now host the teacher in his home. He responds to Jesus immediately with happiness and welcomes Jesus to stay with him. Although Jesus has clearly made a deep impression on him, the crowd disapproves because they know that Zacchaeus is a sinner. Yet, the heart of Zacchaeus is changed after meeting Jesus. He promises to give half of his wealth to the poor and to pay back fourfold whatever he has swindled from others. His faith in Jesus and his transformed life prepare him to respond to the invitation to enter the kingdom of God.

Jesus says to him, "Today salvation has come to this house." Jesus is the Savior of the outcasts and sinners. Because Zacchaeus has accepted the invitation to a relationship with Jesus, God has delivered him and brought him new life. As a descendant of Abraham, Zacchaeus is receiving God's ancient promises being brought by Jesus. The final verse summarizes this mission: "The Son of Man came to seek out and to save the lost." The account of Zacchaeus offers a model for this work of seeking out the lost and bringing them back to God. Jesus is the agent of God's rescue mission, the mission illustrated in Jesus' parables of the lost sheep, the lost coin, and the prodigal son. Jesus' passionate desire is to initiate relationships with those who have strayed from God and to proclaim salvation for those who respond with faith and generosity.

Reflection and discussion

• Why might Jesus have been particularly attracted to Zacchaeus, and why did Jesus single him out to stay at his house? What might Jesus and Zacchaeus have discussed over dinner that evening?

• What are some similarities between the disapproving crowd in this scene and the older brother of the prodigal son?

Prayer

Son of Man, you came to seek out and save the lost. Come into my life as you stayed in the house of Zacchaeus. Open my heart to be generous to those in need, and show me how to use the resources you have given me for your service.

"When he returned, having received royal power, he ordered these slaves,
to whom he had given the money, to be summoned so that
he might find out what they had gained by trading." Luke 19:15

Stewardship While Awaiting the Kingdom

LUKE 19:11–27 ¹¹*As they were listening to this, he went on to tell a parable, because he was near Jerusalem, and because they supposed that the kingdom of God was to appear immediately.* ¹²*So he said, "A nobleman went to a distant country to get royal power for himself and then return.* ¹³*He summoned ten of his slaves, and gave them ten pounds, and said to them, 'Do business with these until I come back.'* ¹⁴*But the citizens of his country hated him and sent a delegation after him, saying, 'We do not want this man to rule over us.'* ¹⁵*When he returned, having received royal power, he ordered these slaves, to whom he had given the money, to be summoned so that he might find out what they had gained by trading.* ¹⁶*The first came forward and said, 'Lord, your pound has made ten more pounds.'* ¹⁷*He said to him, 'Well done, good slave! Because you have been trustworthy in a very small thing, take charge of ten cities.'* ¹⁸*Then the second came, saying, 'Lord, your pound has made five pounds.'* ¹⁹*He said to him, 'And you, rule over five cities.'* ²⁰*Then the other came, saying, 'Lord, here is your pound. I wrapped it up in a piece of cloth,* ²¹*for I was afraid of you,* *because you are a harsh man; you take what you did not deposit, and reap what you did not sow.' ²²He said to him, 'I will judge you by your own words, you wicked slave! You knew, did you, that I was a harsh man, taking what I did not deposit and reaping what I did not sow? ²³Why then did you not put my money into the bank? Then when I returned, I could have collected it with interest.' ²⁴He said to the bystanders, 'Take the pound from him and give it to the one who has ten pounds.' ²⁵(And they said to him, 'Lord, he has ten pounds!') ²⁶'I tell you, to all those who have, more will be given; but from those who have nothing, even what they have will be taken away. ²⁷But as for these enemies of mine who did not want me to be king over them—bring them here and slaughter them in my presence.'"*

As Jesus draws near Jerusalem, many of his disciples falsely assume that the kingdom of God is about to appear in its fullness and be established in Jerusalem. Their expectations likely include the overthrow of Roman rule and the restoration of the kingdom to Israel. Jesus addresses these false hopes by telling this parable, a narrative which assumes that there will be an interim period between the inauguration of the kingdom by Jesus and its future fullness. In this interim period, which the Acts of the Apostles will show to be the age of the church, the disciples have responsibilities to carry out while they await the establishment of God's reign in its fullness. They must serve faithfully until the Son of Man comes in glory.

As the parable begins, a nobleman is preparing to leave his own country to travel to a distant land where he will obtain royal power and then return as king. But before he departs, he gives responsibilities to ten of his slaves. He divides ten pounds among them, instructing them to use the money to establish businesses while he is away as a preparation for their being given greater responsibilities when he comes back. When the nobleman returns as king, he summons those slaves to whom he has given the pounds to see what return they have gained on the money. Coming forward, one by one, the servants report on their earnings while their master was away. The one who earned ten pounds is praised and put in charge of ten cities. The one who earned five pounds is also commended and given five cities to rule. But the one who hid his pound is severely rebuked. When the king asks him why he merely hid the money, he admits his fear of the king, thinking he is severe and unjust.

The slave's excuse is ludicrous. If he really believes his master is so harsh, then all the more reason he should have made an effort to do something beneficial with the money. Or perhaps the slave is lying about his perception of his master's character to excuse his own lack of response. Either way, the slave has failed his king. Clearly, this slave does not know his master, and his view of authority is totally mistaken. As a result, his one pound is given to the most faithful slave, while the unfaithful one is left with nothing.

This third servant represents disciples who fail to see God's gifts as acts of his grace, extended to them in kindness, to be used in his service. Because they see their master as harsh and demanding, they paralyze themselves and do not act. They refuse to respond to him and are left with nothing because they never truly knew or trusted God.

Finally, the parable points to the king's subjects who hate him and do not want him to reign over them. These opponents of the kingdom receive a severe judgment and are destroyed. This image serves as a solemn warning that those who reject the reign of Jesus will not be part of the kingdom which he establishes. As Jesus nears Jerusalem, he is not going to immediately establish God's kingdom in its fullness. Rather, he is on the way to the "exodus" that he will accomplish there, his journey to God through suffering and death. The parable is both a promise and a warning that Jesus will be gone for some time and that on his return he will evaluate the stewardship of all.

Reflection and discussion

• What promises do I find in this parable? What warnings do I find there?

• Is my view of Jesus more like that of the faithful servants or of the unrespon-sive one? Do I view him as stern, demanding, severe, and paralyzing, or as kind and generous with his gifts and rewards?

• As we live in the interim, between the saving life, death, and resurrection of Jesus and the completion of his reign over creation, what is my role? What determines whether I am a faithful or unfaithful servant?

• What gifts and resources have I been given to serve the church? How should I put them to use before the Master returns?

Prayer

Lord and Master, you have given me gifts to be used in the service of your church. As I pray for the coming of your kingdom, may I work to prove myself trustworthy by faithfully using the resources you have given me.

As he was now approaching the path down from the Mount of Olives,
the whole multitude of the disciples began to praise God joyfully
with a loud voice for all the deeds of power that they had seen. Luke 19:37

Jesus Comes to Jerusalem

LUKE 19:28–48 ²⁸*After he had said this, he went on ahead, going up to Jerusalem.*

²⁹*When he had come near Bethphage and Bethany, at the place called the Mount of Olives, he sent two of the disciples,* ³⁰*saying, "Go into the village ahead of you, and as you enter it you will find tied there a colt that has never been ridden. Untie it and bring it here.* ³¹*If anyone asks you, 'Why are you untying it?' just say this, 'The Lord needs it.'"* ³²*So those who were sent departed and found it as he had told them.* ³³*As they were untying the colt, its owners asked them, "Why are you untying the colt?"* ³⁴*They said, "The Lord needs it."* ³⁵*Then they brought it to Jesus; and after throwing their cloaks on the colt, they set Jesus on it.* ³⁶*As he rode along, people kept spreading their cloaks on the road.* ³⁷*As he was now approaching the path down from the Mount of Olives, the whole multitude of the disciples began to praise God joyfully with a loud voice for all the deeds of power that they had seen,* ³⁸*saying,*

"Blessed is the king
who comes in the name of the Lord!

76

Peace in heaven,
and glory in the highest heaven!"
[39]*Some of the Pharisees in the crowd said to him, "Teacher, order your disciples to stop." *[40]*He answered, "I tell you, if these were silent, the stones would shout out."*

[41]*As he came near and saw the city, he wept over it, *[42]*saying, "If you, even you, had only recognized on this day the things that make for peace! But now they are hidden from your eyes. *[43]*Indeed, the days will come upon you, when your enemies will set up ramparts around you and surround you, and hem you in on every side. *[44]*They will crush you to the ground, you and your children within you, and they will not leave within you one stone upon another; because you did not recognize the time of your visitation from God."*

[45]*Then he entered the temple and began to drive out those who were selling things there; *[46]*and he said, "It is written,*
'My house shall be a house of prayer';
but you have made it a den of robbers."
[47]*Every day he was teaching in the temple. The chief priests, the scribes, and the leaders of the people kept looking for a way to kill him; *[48]*but they did not find anything they could do, for all the people were spellbound by what they heard.*

Jesus makes the final climb up to Jerusalem, and before he enters the city, he passes the villages of Bethphage and Bethany. He sends two of his disciples into one of the towns to obtain a colt for his entry into the city. If anyone asks why they are untying it, Jesus says that their reply, "The Lord needs it," will be a sufficient response. The fact that they found things "as he had told them" emphasizes that Jesus has knowledge and control over the details of the coming events of his passion.

As the animal is brought to Jesus, the disciples place their cloaks on the colt for a saddle and set Jesus upon the beast, while other people spread their garments along the road he will travel. Jesus' final journey, from the Mount of Olives to the walls of Jerusalem, recalls the prophetic language of Zechariah in which God invites Jerusalem to rejoice greatly and shout aloud, "Lo, your king comes to you; triumphant and victorious is he, humble and riding on a donkey, on a colt, the foal of a donkey" (Zech 9:9).

As Jesus descends the Mount and ascends to Jerusalem, the multitude sings joyful praise to God for all the saving deeds they have witnessed in Jesus: "Blessed is the king who comes in the name of the Lord!" Their cry is full of hope as they welcome Jesus as the Messiah. When the religious leaders ask Jesus to quiet the crowd, he replies that if these were silent, even creation would cry out in acclamation. Yet their joyful praise will soon turn to wails of bitter disappointment. A donkey now bears him as king, but soon he will carry his own cross. He triumphantly approaches the gates of the great city, but in a few days he will be led outside the city gates for crucifixion.

As Jesus approaches Jerusalem, he begins to weep over the city (verses 41–42). His tears express his sadness, anger, and frustration for the nation's rejection of God's message and his Messiah. Speaking like a prophet, he declares divine judgment upon the city for its failures to respond to his call to repentance. His lament is reminiscent of Jeremiah's grief over the coming exile (Jer 6:6–21) or Isaiah's declaration of the coming siege of Jerusalem (Isa 29:1–4). The disastrous collapse of the city is the tragic consequence of rejecting the gospel's message of peace and non-violence. Jerusalem, the city of peace, does not know what to do in order to secure its peace. It will be besieged by its enemies who will dash it to the ground, not leaving one stone upon another (verses 43–44). Indeed, in AD 70, the Romans will destroy the temple, tear down the walls of the city, and level and burn houses and buildings.

In another prophetic action, Jesus enters the temple and begins to drive out the merchants who are benefitting financially from Israel's worship. As God's Messiah, he takes possession of the temple, seeking to cleanse it from impurities and declaring what it should be. Jesus first cites Isaiah, expressing the divine hope that the temple will be "a house of prayer for all peoples" (Isa 56:7). He contrasts what the temple should have been, a house of prayer for Israelites and foreigners, and what it has become, a commercial center to benefit the powerful priestly aristocracy. Jesus then cites Jeremiah, condemning those who have made the temple "a den of robbers" (Jer 7:11). The religious leaders have become robbers, enriching themselves from the temple worship. Through this prophetic action, Jesus symbolically expresses his protest of those who would use God's temple for profit rather than prayer. For this reason, the religious leaders sought a way to put Jesus to death, yet they were unable to seize him because of his popularity among the people.

Reflection and discussion

• What do you see, hear, and feel emotionally as you enter imaginatively into the scene of Jesus' entry into Jerusalem?

• Why does Jesus weep as he comes near Jerusalem? How does our society today fail to recognize "the things that make for peace"?

• Luke tells us that all the people were "spellbound" as they listen to Jesus. When have I been fascinated and captivated by Jesus?

Prayer

Humble Messiah, blessed are you who comes in the name of the Lord. I praise your glory and listen spellbound to your word. May my worship be always cleansed from self-interest and forever sing your praises.

SUGGESTIONS FOR FACILITATORS, GROUP SESSION 4

1. Welcome group members and ask if anyone has any questions, announcements, or requests.

2. You may want to pray this prayer as a group:

God of all people, help us to recognize the presence of your kingdom among us as we await the fullness of your kingdom when your Son comes in glory. May we always respond to you with gratitude for the healing, forgiveness, and salvation you continually offer us. Keep us on guard so that we will not cause others to stumble, and open our hearts to be generous with the resources you have given us for your service. As we continue to listen to your word through the life and teachings of Jesus, increase our faith so that we can entrust our lives to him.

3. Ask one or more of the following questions:
   • What is the most difficult part of this study for you?
   • What insights stand out to you from the lessons this week?

4. Discuss lessons 13 through 18. Choose one or more of the questions for reflection and discussion from each lesson to discuss as a group. You may want to ask group members which question was most challenging or helpful to them as you review each lesson.

5. Keep the discussion moving, but allow time for the questions that provoke the most discussion. Encourage the group members to use "I" language in their responses.

6. After talking over each lesson, instruct group members to complete lessons 19 through 24 on their own during the six days before the next group meeting. They should write out their own answers to the questions as preparation for next week's session.

7. Ask the group what encouragement they need for the coming week. Ask the members to pray for the needs of one another during the week.

8. Conclude by praying aloud together the prayer at the end of one of the lessons discussed. You may choose to conclude the prayer by asking members to pray aloud any requests they may have.

"Teacher, we know that you are right in what you say and teach, and you show deference to no one, but teach the way of God in accordance with truth." Luke 20:21

Questions and Controversies in the Temple

LUKE 20:1–26 *¹One day, as he was teaching the people in the temple and telling the good news, the chief priests and the scribes came with the elders ²and said to him, "Tell us, by what authority are you doing these things? Who is it who gave you this authority?" ³He answered them, "I will also ask you a question, and you tell me: ⁴Did the baptism of John come from heaven, or was it of human origin?" ⁵They discussed it with one another, saying, "If we say, 'From heaven,' he will say, 'Why did you not believe him?' ⁶But if we say, 'Of human origin,' all the people will stone us; for they are convinced that John was a prophet." ⁷So they answered that they did not know where it came from. ⁸Then Jesus said to them, "Neither will I tell you by what authority I am doing these things."*

⁹He began to tell the people this parable: "A man planted a vineyard, and leased it to tenants, and went to another country for a long time. ¹⁰When the season came, he sent a slave to the tenants in order that they might give him his share of the produce of the vineyard; but the tenants beat him and sent him away empty-handed. [11]*Next he sent another slave; that one also they beat and insulted and sent away empty-handed.* [12]*And he sent still a third; this one also they wounded and threw out.* [13]*Then the owner of the vineyard said, 'What shall I do? I will send my beloved son; perhaps they will respect him.'* [14]*But when the tenants saw him, they discussed it among themselves and said, 'This is the heir; let us kill him so that the inheritance may be ours.'* [15]*So they threw him out of the vineyard and killed him. What then will the owner of the vineyard do to them?* [16]*He will come and destroy those tenants and give the vineyard to others."* *When they heard this, they said, "Heaven forbid!"* [17]*But he looked at them and said, "What then does this text mean:*

> *'The stone that the builders rejected*
> *has become the cornerstone'?*

[18]*Everyone who falls on that stone will be broken to pieces; and it will crush anyone on whom it falls."* [19]*When the scribes and chief priests realized that he had told this parable against them, they wanted to lay hands on him at that very hour, but they feared the people.*

[20]*So they watched him and sent spies who pretended to be honest, in order to trap him by what he said, so as to hand him over to the jurisdiction and authority of the governor.* [21]*So they asked him, "Teacher, we know that you are right in what you say and teach, and you show deference to no one, but teach the way of God in accordance with truth.* [22]*Is it lawful for us to pay taxes to the emperor, or not?"* [23]*But he perceived their craftiness and said to them,* [24]*"Show me a denarius. Whose head and whose title does it bear?" They said, "The emperor's."* [25]*He said to them, "Then give to the emperor the things that are the emperor's, and to God the things that are God's."* [26]*And they were not able in the presence of the people to trap him by what he said; and being amazed by his answer, they became silent.*

As Jesus spends his days teaching in the courtyard of the temple, he enters into a series of controversies with the religious leadership of Jerusalem. They test Jesus personally, politically, and theologically, in order to catch him in error. Jesus shows great skill in avoiding a trap, while at the same time creating traps for his opponents and reducing them to silence. The entire series of controversies points to Jesus as the source of wisdom for God's people.

After seeing Jesus cleanse the temple and hearing him teach the people there, the temple leaders challenge Jesus to name the source of his authority (verse 2). Rather than reply directly, Jesus employs a common rabbinical technique and poses a counterquestion about John the Baptist. The gospel has already shown how the ministries of John and Jesus were linked. Since the people are convinced that John was a prophet sent from God, the religious leaders cannot deny the source of John's authority without incurring the wrath of the people (verse 6). But if they accept that John's ministry is from God, they must also acknowledge the divine authority of Jesus, the one to whom John pointed the way. Faced with this quandary, the authorities opt out of the discussion and expose their lack of sincerity and conviction.

Jesus' parable of the vineyard recalls a parable from Isaiah in which the prophet had offered the vineyard as an image for God's people. In Jesus' version, the owner of the vineyard sends slaves to collect the produce of the vineyard, but they are each mistreated by the tenants and sent away, just as the leaders of Israel had rejected the prophets. And when the vineyard owner finally sends his beloved son, they kill him, hoping to receive his inheritance. Jesus implies that he is the rejected son who will be put to death by those now holding authority over God's people. The role of tenant of God's people is taken away from the scribes and chief priests of Israel and given to others—namely, the apostles and leadership of the church.

As Jesus concludes the application of his parable, he cites Psalm 118:22. Jesus is the stone that was rejected by the religious leaders of Israel but exalted by God to the place of honor (verse 17). He is the cornerstone of a new edifice, the new temple where God will be present, the church that will be built on the foundation of the apostles. The coming destruction of Jerusalem and its temple in AD 70 make this metaphor especially fitting for the age in which Luke wrote and particularly poignant for his readers.

In the next controversy account, the religious authorities send spies to trap Jesus over the particularly sensitive issue of paying taxes to Rome. The tax expressed in concrete economic terms the subjugation of the people of Israel to the Romans. The spies use the familiar either/or tactic on Jesus. If Jesus advocates paying the taxes, he would be legitimizing foreign, pagan rule over God's people. If he opposes paying the taxes, he would be sowing the seeds of rebellion against the empire. In asking them to show him a coin, Jesus forces his antagonists to admit that they carry around signs of Roman domination every day. Since they live under the empire and use its currency, they should pay its tax. Those things that bear the image of the emperor belong to the emperor, but what bears the image of God belongs to God. Since all people are made in God's image, one's fundamental allegiance is to God. While acknowledging the legitimate role of government authority, Jesus asserts that everyone must honor God and that everything ultimately belongs to him.

Reflection and discussion

• How does Jesus avoid the traps that his opponents have set for him?

• What are some of the issues people face when choosing between their allegiance to their government and to God?

• Read Romans 12:1-2 and 13:1-2. What do these verses add to my discernment about my obligations to the government and to God?

Prayer

Heavenly Father, you are Lord of all the earth and your authority extends to all people. I submit my life to your reign and pray that your will be done on earth as it is in heaven.

"The fact that the dead are raised Moses himself showed, in the story about the bush, where he speaks of the Lord as the God of Abraham, the God of Isaac, and the God of Jacob. Now he is God not of the dead, but of the living; for to him all of them are alive." Luke 20:37–38

Teaching about Resurrected Life

LUKE 20:27–40 *²⁷Some Sadducees, those who say there is no resurrection, came to him ²⁸and asked him a question, "Teacher, Moses wrote for us that if a man's brother dies, leaving a wife but no children, the man shall marry the widow and raise up children for his brother. ²⁹Now there were seven brothers; the first married, and died childless; ³⁰then the second ³¹and the third married her, and so in the same way all seven died childless. ³²Finally the woman also died. ³³In the resurrection, therefore, whose wife will the woman be? For the seven had married her."*

³⁴Jesus said to them, "Those who belong to this age marry and are given in marriage; ³⁵but those who are considered worthy of a place in that age and in the resurrection from the dead neither marry nor are given in marriage. ³⁶Indeed they cannot die anymore, because they are like angels and are children of God, being children of the resurrection. ³⁷And the fact that the dead are raised Moses himself showed, in the story about the bush, where he speaks of the Lord as the God of Abraham, the God of Isaac, and the God of Jacob. ³⁸Now he is God not of the dead, but of the living; for to him all of them are alive." ³⁹Then some of the scribes answered, "Teacher, you have spoken well." ⁴⁰For they no longer dared to ask him another question.

In a further attempt to entrap Jesus, some Sadducees confront him as he is teaching in the temple's courtyard. As one of the many forms of Jewish belief and practice in the first century, the Sadducees were socially aristocratic and religiously conservative. They considered only the written Torah as authoritative Scripture and thus rejected many ideas held by other Jewish groups, such as belief in the resurrection of the dead. These Sadducees have heard that Jesus teaches that men and women will be raised from the dead, and they pose a situation to him designed to demonstrate the absurdity of believing in the resurrection.

The Sadducees propose the state of affairs in which one woman had seven husbands in succession. Israel's law of levirate marriage stipulated that if a man dies without leaving a son, one of his brothers should marry his widow and beget a son to carry on his deceased brother's name (Deut 25:5–6). In this bizarre scenario proposed by the Sadducees, all seven brothers married the woman and all seven died without leaving any children. So the Sadducees ask the question about the life of resurrection: "Whose wife will the woman be?" The absurdity of the woman's dilemma is designed to show the futility of hope in resurrected life. Convinced that no adequate answer can be found, the Sadducees think they have Jesus trapped by his own teaching.

Jesus responds to the Sadducees by contrasting the present age, in which people marry and are given in marriage, and the age of the resurrection, in which people neither marry nor are given in marriage (verses 34–35). The resurrection is different from the present life, so much so that the situation posed by the Sadducees does not apply. Since the risen life is immortal, marriage is no longer necessary, because there is no need to have children and beget heirs. Life in the age to come may be compared to the life of angels, who do not marry, have children, or die. The risen life is not only different than the present life, but it is a much greater kind of existence.

Jesus shows the Sadducees that Scripture points to belief in the resurrection of the dead by referring to a passage from the Torah. When God speaks of himself as the God of Abraham, the God of Isaac, and the God of Jacob, he shows himself to be the God of the living and not the dead (Exod 3:6). God lives in a personal and continuing relationship with Israel's ancestors, even though they died centuries before God made this revelation to Moses. A relationship with God, built on covenant and promise, does not end with this life, but continues and reaches its fulfillment in the next.

Jesus has silenced all his opponents. They no longer dare to ask him any more questions. He has stood against the challenges of all the major ruling groups within Judaism: the Pharisees, chief priests, scribes, elders, and Sadducees. Faced with personal and political issues, and finally with the theological challenge of resurrected life, he has prevailed with the truth of his instructions. Jesus is the superior teacher of Israel.

Reflection and discussion

• How does Jesus demonstrate the irrelevance of the future scenario posed by the Sadducees?

• The Sadducees refused to recognize God's power to transform created reality through resurrection. Why is the resurrection of the dead the hallmark of Christian belief?

• In what ways does my belief in the future resurrection affect how I see the world and life within it today?

Prayer

God of Abraham, Isaac, and Jacob, you are the God of the living, and you have created all people to share life with you forever. Keep me faithful to your purpose in creating me as I await the life of the world to come.

"So make up your minds not to prepare your defense in advance; for I will give you words and a wisdom that none of your opponents will be able to withstand or contradict." Luke 21:14–15

Destruction and Persecution to Come

LUKE 21:1–19 ¹*He looked up and saw rich people putting their gifts into the treasury;* ²*he also saw a poor widow put in two small copper coins.* ³*He said, "Truly I tell you, this poor widow has put in more than all of them;* ⁴*for all of them have contributed out of their abundance, but she out of her poverty has put in all she had to live on."*

⁵*When some were speaking about the temple, how it was adorned with beautiful stones and gifts dedicated to God, he said,* ⁶*"As for these things that you see, the days will come when not one stone will be left upon another; all will be thrown down."*

⁷*They asked him, "Teacher, when will this be, and what will be the sign that this is about to take place?"* ⁸*And he said, "Beware that you are not led astray; for many will come in my name and say, 'I am he!' and, 'The time is near!' Do not go after them.*

⁹*"When you hear of wars and insurrections, do not be terrified; for these things must take place first, but the end will not follow immediately."* ¹⁰*Then he said to them, "Nation will rise against nation, and kingdom against kingdom;* ¹¹*there will be great earthquakes, and in various places famines and plagues; and there will be dreadful portents and great signs from heaven.*

¹²*"But before all this occurs, they will arrest you and persecute you; they will hand you over to synagogues and prisons, and you will be brought before kings and governors because of my name.* ¹³*This will give you an opportunity to testify.* ¹⁴*So make up your minds not to prepare your defense in advance;* ¹⁵*for I will give you words and a wisdom that none of your opponents will be able to withstand or contradict.* ¹⁶*You will be betrayed even by parents and brothers, by relatives and friends; and they will put some of you to death.* ¹⁷*You will be hated by all because of my name.* ¹⁸*But not a hair of your head will perish.* ¹⁹*By your endurance you will gain your souls."*

As Jesus continues his teaching in the courtyard of the temple, he is in a position to observe wealthy people depositing their large and clanging coins into the receptacles used to collect offerings for financing temple worship. He also notices, in contrast, a poor widow dropping two small, chinking coins into the container. Her coins are the smallest currency available, made of copper and worth a minimal amount. Although the woman does not give much, Jesus says that it is as if she has given everything she possesses. In terms of real cost, she has given more than all the others. Jesus explains that the others give out of their abundance, but the woman offers her whole life. She serves from the heart and not to self-advantage.

In the shadow of Israel's temple, some of the disciples marvel at its white marble stones and the beauty of its decorative gifts. They are rightly proud of this focal point for the nation of Israel. Yet, Jesus says, "Not one stone will be left upon another; all will be thrown down." Although the temple looks impressive now, Jesus knows that in time it will be reduced to rubble. This prediction of the temple's destruction and the disciples' questions about when it will occur lead to Jesus' discourse about the destruction of the temple and the glorious coming of the Son of Man. The destruction of Jerusalem will not be the end of the world, but Jesus' interweaving of these two events makes Jesus' discourse difficult to interpret.

The destruction of the city and its temple occurred in AD 70, about four decades after the final days of Jesus' ministry. As he speaks about the coming destruction, Jesus also warns his disciples about false messiahs and those claiming that the end is near (verse 8). He tells his disciples not to be deceived by these claims and not to be led away by pretenders. During the interval between Jesus' departure and his return, which Acts shows to be the age of the church, the disciples will need discernment and guidance in order to continually respond to God's plan.

To his list of occurrences that precede the end, Jesus adds the social tumult of wars, rebellions, and international conflicts. In addition to human violence, there will be natural disasters in the form of earthquakes, famines, plagues, and cosmic portents. As dreadful as these events may be, disciples should not be terrified and think that they indicate the end of the world.

Yet, even before all of these things happen, the disciples can expect to experience persecution. Many will be arrested and imprisoned, and some will even be put to death because of their faith. The Acts of the Apostles shows that many disciples were brought before both Jewish authorities and Roman officials because of the name of Jesus. But this persecution will provide disciples with "an opportunity to testify" (verse 13), to explain their commitment to Jesus. And their witness will be aided by the words and wisdom of the Holy Spirit who will be given by the risen Jesus to his church.

Despite the coming persecution and all the costs of discipleship, Jesus offers security and confidence to his disciples. He assures them that they will not face final destruction, because no persecutor can deprive them of eternal life (verse 18). Their steadfast perseverance, clinging to their faith through the trial, will lead to their salvation. Remaining in Jesus means life, even in the face of death.

Reflection and discussion

• In what way does the poor widow demonstrate that the size of a gift is not always indicative of the sacrifice? What has shown me that little gifts are sometimes in fact the biggest gifts of all?

• How did the Jewish disciples of Jesus feel about the temple? How might its destruction seem like the end of the world?

• Jesus warns his disciples not to be deceived, led astray, or terrified by either human violence or natural disasters. What might be the meaning of his words for our own times?

• Jesus promises to give his disciples the right words and the wisdom needed to bear witness to him. When have I been aware of this gift?

Prayer

Good Teacher, I know that everything that gives me security in this world will eventually be destroyed, but your word and your promises continue forever. Help me to trust in you to preserve me from all harm.

"Be on guard so that your hearts are not weighed down
with dissipation and drunkenness and the worries of this life,
and that day catch you unexpectedly, like a trap." Luke 21:34–35

The Need for Watchfulness

LUKE 21:20–38 ²⁰*"When you see Jerusalem surrounded by armies, then know that its desolation has come near.* ²¹*Then those in Judea must flee to the mountains, and those inside the city must leave it, and those out in the country must not enter it;* ²²*for these are days of vengeance, as a fulfillment of all that is written.* ²³*Woe to those who are pregnant and to those who are nursing infants in those days! For there will be great distress on the earth and wrath against this people;* ²⁴*they will fall by the edge of the sword and be taken away as captives among all nations; and Jerusalem will be trampled on by the Gentiles, until the times of the Gentiles are fulfilled.*

²⁵*"There will be signs in the sun, the moon, and the stars, and on the earth distress among nations confused by the roaring of the sea and the waves.* ²⁶*People will faint from fear and foreboding of what is coming upon the world, for the powers of the heavens will be shaken.* ²⁷*Then they will see 'the Son of Man coming in a cloud' with power and great glory.* ²⁸*Now when these things begin to take place, stand up and raise your heads, because your redemption is drawing near."*

²⁹*Then he told them a parable: "Look at the fig tree and all the trees;* ³⁰*as soon as they sprout leaves you can see for yourselves and know that summer is already near.* ³¹*So also, when you see these things taking place, you know that the king-*

dom of God is near. ³²*Truly I tell you, this generation will not pass away until all things have taken place.* ³³*Heaven and earth will pass away, but my words will not pass away.*

³⁴*"Be on guard so that your hearts are not weighed down with dissipation and drunkenness and the worries of this life, and that day catch you unexpectedly,* ³⁵*like a trap. For it will come upon all who live on the face of the whole earth.* ³⁶*Be alert at all times, praying that you may have the strength to escape all these things that will take place, and to stand before the Son of Man."*

³⁷*Every day he was teaching in the temple, and at night he would go out and spend the night on the Mount of Olives, as it was called.* ³⁸*And all the people would get up early in the morning to listen to him in the temple.*

As Jesus describes the upcoming devastation of Jerusalem and its temple, he is offering a preview of the end of the age and his glorious return. What happens as the destruction of Jerusalem in AD 70 approaches is a foretaste of what will happen as the end nears. As Jesus answers the short-term question of the disciples about the end of the temple, he also sets up a long-term anticipation of the end of the world. He wants to make clear that the coming destruction of the city, the terror of which he vividly describes, is not yet the end-time.

When the armies of Rome attack, the walled city of Jerusalem will be surrounded by encamped soldiers. Those living in the area of Judea should flee to the mountains for protection. Those living in the city should escape if they are able, and those working in the countryside should not try to reenter the city gates. Just like the siege of Jerusalem by the Babylonians and the destruction of the first temple six centuries before, it will be a time of great devastation. Many will be killed and many taken captive, and as in all wars, women and children will suffer the most.

As the prophets of old warned, the devastation of the city and its temple will be a result of Israel's infidelity to God's covenant. The consequence of not walking in the way of God will be the destruction of the gifts God's people have received in covenant. Jesus speaks as a great prophet, addressing the coming period of judgment upon God's people. His words are part of an escalating pattern of prophetic oracles expressing infidelity, judgment, and destruction of God's people and their religious institutions. The Babylonian conquest foretells the Roman conquest, and the Roman conquest prefigures the final judgment of the world and the return of Christ.

"The Son of Man coming in a cloud" is an image from the prophet Daniel which Jesus invokes as referring to his own majestic coming (verses 26–28). The Son of Man comes with great power and glory, and he receives the authority of God's kingdom. His appearance with cosmic signs represents the approach of the world's consummation. While many will cower and faint from fear, the disciples of Jesus may stand up and raise their heads, for their complete redemption from the fallen world is drawing near. It will be a time of joyful fulfillment, when all of God's promises to his people will be fully realized.

Jesus' words that "this generation will not pass away until all things have taken place" does not mean that the end of the world will happen in the lifetime of Jesus' listeners. Rather, each generation must live as if it will. Jesus told his disciples that wars and insurrections, earthquakes and famines, persecution and trial, and the destruction of Jerusalem and the temple will happen within their own generation. Yet, each generation must know that similar events will occur within each generation between the devastation of Jerusalem and the coming of the Son of Man in a cloud.

Jesus' focus is not on when he will return but on how his disciples should await his return. Nothing can enable us to predict his final coming very far in advance, so we must live in constant anticipation, as if every moment were as important as our last moment of life in this world. Living with this kind of watchful alertness and prayerful vigilance will enable us to live faithfully until he comes again.

Reflection and discussion

• What comfort and encouragement does Jesus offer to his disciples in the midst of the tribulations to come?

• Which of the signs about which Jesus spoke have occurred continually in each generation during the age of the church, between the resurrection of Jesus and his future coming in glory?

• What are my expectations about the coming of Jesus? What do I have in mind when I pray "thy kingdom come"?

• How does Jesus urge his disciples to live during the age of his church? What are the challenges I encounter in trying to live in this way?

Prayer

Lord Jesus, I know that heaven and earth will pass away, but your words will remain. As I live in expectant hope for your final coming, give me the grace to live each day focused on your promises.

"I have eagerly desired to eat this Passover with you before I suffer;
for I tell you, I will not eat it until it is fulfilled in the kingdom of God."
Luke 22:15–16

From Passover to Passion

LUKE 22:1–38 ¹*Now the festival of Unleavened Bread, which is called the Passover, was near.* ²*The chief priests and the scribes were looking for a way to put Jesus to death, for they were afraid of the people.*

³*Then Satan entered into Judas called Iscariot, who was one of the twelve;* ⁴*he went away and conferred with the chief priests and officers of the temple police about how he might betray him to them.* ⁵*They were greatly pleased and agreed to give him money.* ⁶*So he consented and began to look for an opportunity to betray him to them when no crowd was present.*

⁷*Then came the day of Unleavened Bread, on which the Passover lamb had to be sacrificed.* ⁸*So Jesus sent Peter and John, saying, "Go and prepare the Passover meal for us that we may eat it."* ⁹*They asked him, "Where do you want us to make preparations for it?"* ¹⁰*"Listen," he said to them, "when you have entered the city, a man carrying a jar of water will meet you; follow him into the house he enters* ¹¹*and say to the owner of the house, 'The teacher asks you, "Where is the guest room, where I may eat the Passover with my disciples?"'* ¹²*He will show you a large room upstairs, already furnished. Make preparations for us there."* ¹³*So they went and found everything as he had told them; and they prepared the Passover meal.*

¹⁴*When the hour came, he took his place at the table, and the apostles with him.* ¹⁵*He said to them, "I have eagerly desired to eat this Passover with you before I suffer;* ¹⁶*for I tell you, I will not eat it until it is fulfilled in the kingdom of God." * ¹⁷*Then he took a cup, and after giving thanks he said, "Take this and divide it among yourselves;* ¹⁸*for I tell you that from now on I will not drink of the fruit of the vine until the kingdom of God comes." * ¹⁹*Then he took a loaf of bread, and when he had given thanks, he broke it and gave it to them, saying, "This is my body, which is given for you. Do this in remembrance of me." * ²⁰*And he did the same with the cup after supper, saying, "This cup that is poured out for you is the new covenant in my blood.*

²¹*"But see, the one who betrays me is with me, and his hand is on the table.* ²²*For the Son of Man is going as it has been determined, but woe to that one by whom he is betrayed!" * ²³*Then they began to ask one another, which one of them it could be who would do this.*

²⁴*A dispute also arose among them as to which one of them was to be regarded as the greatest.* ²⁵*But he said to them, "The kings of the Gentiles lord it over them; and those in authority over them are called benefactors.* ²⁶*But not so with you; rather the greatest among you must become like the youngest, and the leader like one who serves.* ²⁷*For who is greater, the one who is at the table or the one who serves? Is it not the one at the table? But I am among you as one who serves.*

²⁸*"You are those who have stood by me in my trials;* ²⁹*and I confer on you, just as my Father has conferred on me, a kingdom,* ³⁰*so that you may eat and drink at my table in my kingdom, and you will sit on thrones judging the twelve tribes of Israel.*

³¹*"Simon, Simon, listen! Satan has demanded to sift all of you like wheat,* ³²*but I have prayed for you that your own faith may not fail; and you, when once you have turned back, strengthen your brothers." * ³³*And he said to him, "Lord, I am ready to go with you to prison and to death!" * ³⁴*Jesus said, "I tell you, Peter, the cock will not crow this day, until you have denied three times that you know me."*

³⁵*He said to them, "When I sent you out without a purse, bag, or sandals, did you lack anything?" They said, "No, not a thing." * ³⁶*He said to them, "But now, the one who has a purse must take it, and likewise a bag. And the one who has no sword must sell his cloak and buy one.* ³⁷*For I tell you, this scripture must be fulfilled in me, 'And he was counted among the lawless'; and indeed what is writ-*

ten about me is being fulfilled." [38] *They said, "Lord, look, here are two swords."*
He replied, "It is enough."

The goal of Jesus' journey to Jerusalem is the accomplishment of "his exodus" on the cross, and there cannot be a new Exodus without a new Passover. So Jesus sent Peter and John to prepare the Passover, which consists of the sacrifice of a lamb in the temple and the eating of a sacrificial meal. This memorial feast, celebrated by the people of Israel since the night before their exodus from Egypt, consisted of the lamb, unleavened bread and wine, and other symbolic foods representing various aspects of Israel's Exodus.

But Jesus celebrates this ancient ritual and transforms it into the sacrificial meal of the new covenant. Jesus explains that he has desired to eat the Passover with his disciples before his death, but that he will not share the meal with them again "until it is fulfilled in the kingdom of God" (verses 15–18). It is particularly appropriate that Jesus should share with his disciples this Passover meal before he accomplishes his own exodus to the Father by way of his sacrificial death. His reference to fulfillment in God's kingdom looks toward the future, to the eternal banquet, when the full effects of Jesus' sacrifice are completed. This meal of the new covenant looks beyond the first deliverance of God's people from Egypt to the final deliverance from everything that holds the human race in bondage.

In anticipation of his sacrificial death on the cross, Jesus takes bread, gives thanks, breaks it and gives it to his disciples, saying, "This is my body, which is given for you." He did the same with the cup of wine, saying, "This cup that is poured out for you is the new covenant in my blood" (verses 19–20). His body given for us in death and his blood shed for our sake are the new sacrificial banquet, the eucharistic sacrifice, by which his disciples continue to join themselves to his sacrifice and experience his redemption. His mission "to proclaim release to captives" and "to let the oppressed go free," announced in the synagogue of Nazareth (4:18), is accomplished on the cross, made present in every Eucharist, and completed when the kingdom of God is established in its fullness at his coming in glory.

In the first Exodus, God entered into a covenant with his newly liberated people on Mount Sinai, establishing an intimate bond with them. This covenant, like all covenants, was consummated with the blood of sacrifice. In the new Exodus, God establishes a new covenant with his people through the sacrifice of Jesus and the shedding of his blood. And in the new Passover, Jesus gives his church the means to remember and renew this covenant as it celebrates the Eucharist until he comes again.

Because meals were powerful expressions of intimacy, friendship, and trust, the fact that Judas betrays the one with whom he has shared this sacred meal is an unspeakable offense (verse 21). What the religious leadership could not accomplish on their own, a way to put Jesus to death, was handed to them by one of Jesus' chosen twelve. Betrayal by an insider means that Jesus can be handed over privately, avoiding the dangerous reaction from the crowds who follow him. Ironically, the disciples' inquiry about the identity of the betrayer is followed by a dispute among them over who is the greatest (verses 23–24). Jesus expresses the folly of such concern, and desires to change the way his disciples think about leadership and importance.

Although the devil had departed after testing Jesus "until an opportune time" (4:13), at the time of the passion, "Satan entered into Judas" (verse 3). In addition, Jesus says to Simon Peter, "Satan has demanded to sift all of you like wheat" (verse 31), indicating that the powers of evil are shaking and testing the apostles, desiring to get them to fall away. In addition to the tragic human choices made during the passion account, the death of Jesus is ultimately a cosmic battle of the greatest magnitude. In mounting a final assault on Jesus, Satan has found a weak link in Judas and Peter, and desires to subvert the entire mission of Jesus as it comes to its climax.

Reflection and discussion

• Why did Jesus speak of a future event, fulfillment in the kingdom of God (verses 16, 18), in the middle of a meal that looked back to the Exodus?

• What are the indications that the Last Supper, the new Passover, is a sacrificial meal associated with Jesus' death? Why did Jesus command his disciples, "Do this in remembrance of me"?

• Which of Jesus' words to his apostles apply most especially to all future leaders of his church?

• In addition to the choices and decisions made by the human actors in the passion account, what indicates that the passion of Jesus is also a great cosmic battle?

Prayer

Lord Jesus, when I eat your body and drink your blood, you offer me a share in the new covenant and instill within me the hope for your kingdom. Help me to resist the temptations of Satan to draw me away from your saving plan.

"Why are you sleeping? Get up and pray that you
may not come into the time of trial." Luke 22:46

Prayer, Betrayal, and Arrest

LUKE 22:39–71 [39]*He came out and went, as was his custom, to the Mount of Olives; and the disciples followed him.* [40]*When he reached the place, he said to them, "Pray that you may not come into the time of trial."* [41]*Then he withdrew from them about a stone's throw, knelt down, and prayed,* [42]*"Father, if you are willing, remove this cup from me; yet, not my will but yours be done."* [43]*Then an angel from heaven appeared to him and gave him strength.* [44]*In his anguish he prayed more earnestly, and his sweat became like great drops of blood falling down on the ground.* [45]*When he got up from prayer, he came to the disciples and found them sleeping because of grief,* [46]*and he said to them, "Why are you sleeping? Get up and pray that you may not come into the time of trial."*

[47]*While he was still speaking, suddenly a crowd came, and the one called Judas, one of the twelve, was leading them. He approached Jesus to kiss him;* [48]*but Jesus said to him, "Judas, is it with a kiss that you are betraying the Son of Man?"* [49]*When those who were around him saw what was coming, they asked, "Lord, should we strike with the sword?"* [50]*Then one of them struck the slave of the high priest and cut off his right ear.* [51]*But Jesus said, "No more of this!" And he touched his ear and healed him.* [52]*Then Jesus said to the chief priests, the officers of the temple police, and the elders who had come for him, "Have you come out with swords and clubs as if I were a bandit?* [53]*When I was with you day after day in the temple, you did not lay hands on me. But this is your hour, and the power of darkness!"*

[54] Then they seized him and led him away, bringing him into the high priest's house. But Peter was following at a distance. [55] When they had kindled a fire in the middle of the courtyard and sat down together, Peter sat among them. [56] Then a servant-girl, seeing him in the firelight, stared at him and said, "This man also was with him." [57] But he denied it, saying, "Woman, I do not know him." [58] A little later someone else, on seeing him, said, "You also are one of them." But Peter said, "Man, I am not!" [59] Then about an hour later still another kept insisting, "Surely this man also was with him; for he is a Galilean." [60] But Peter said, "Man, I do not know what you are talking about!" At that moment, while he was still speaking, the cock crowed. [61] The Lord turned and looked at Peter. Then Peter remembered the word of the Lord, how he had said to him, "Before the cock crows today, you will deny me three times." [62] And he went out and wept bitterly.

[63] Now the men who were holding Jesus began to mock him and beat him; [64] they also blindfolded him and kept asking him, "Prophesy! Who is it that struck you?" [65] They kept heaping many other insults on him.

[66] When day came, the assembly of the elders of the people, both chief priests and scribes, gathered together, and they brought him to their council. [67] They said, "If you are the Messiah, tell us." He replied, "If I tell you, you will not believe; [68] and if I question you, you will not answer. [69] But from now on the Son of Man will be seated at the right hand of the power of God." [70] All of them asked, "Are you, then, the Son of God?" He said to them, "You say that I am." [71] Then they said, "What further testimony do we need? We have heard it ourselves from his own lips!"

Throughout the gospel, Luke has shown Jesus at prayer, especially at the most critical moments of decision. As he prepares to face his arrest and death, Jesus is praying at a place he visited often on the Mount of Olives. Luke describes Jesus' prayerful dependence on his Father, his submission to God's will, and his great agony and struggle as he faces his final hours. God answers his prayer, not by delivering him from death, but by giving him strength to face the coming ordeal. Jesus urges his disciples to pray also, so that they will persevere and not defect as Satan desires. Although they fail in the short term, they eventually learn from the example of Jesus and become the prayerful community dramatically portrayed in the Acts of the Apostles.

Judas knows where Jesus can be found at night because he is accustomed to praying in a certain place on the Mount of Olives. Judas guides a crowd of Jesus' opponents to him and identifies Jesus by attempting to kiss him. Jesus does not attempt to flee, but those around Jesus want to defend him. When one of them responds with violence, Jesus stops him and heals the severed ear of the slave. He points to the fact that his arrest would not hold up to public scrutiny because they have come under the cover of darkness bearing swords and clubs, when they could have arrested him publicly and peaceably when he was teaching daily in the temple courtyard. The darkness and arms of violence express the domain of evil. For a time, "the power of darkness" will prevail (verse 53). This is the opportune time that Satan had been waiting for (4:13). But even though Satan may have his hour in the cosmic struggle as the crowd chooses darkness, it is only so that the plan of God can come to fulfillment.

The response of Jesus and that of Peter demonstrate a strong contrast. Jesus submits to arrest because he has prepared in prayer, but Peter fails his temptation because he has not prayed. Satan, who has demanded to sift the disciples like wheat, tests Peter through the three questions addressed to him in the courtyard of the high priest's house. Only Luke's gospel mentions that Jesus turned from his trial to look at Peter, just as Peter was denying him and as the cock crowed (verse 61). This look of Jesus creates in Peter a more personal realization of his failure and begins the process of his remorse.

In contrast to Peter's denials, Jesus boldly proclaims his true identity to the council in Jerusalem. In the light of day, Jesus proclaims that "from now on the Son of Man will be seated at the right hand of the power of God" (verse 69). His enthronement in glory is the result of his passion and resurrection. He is indeed the Messiah, Son of Man, and Son of God. From the side of the Father he will grant the blessings of salvation and the gift of the Spirit upon the church. His brave and open witness is the testimony the council needs, and it is the cause of his own conviction.

Reflection and discussion

• What can I learn from the prayer of Jesus on the Mount of Olives?

• When have I denied or downplayed my association with Jesus? What has led me to minimize my discipleship?

• How do I decide when to boldly speak up for what is right and when to remain silent?

Prayer

Son of God, you submitted your life to your Father's will in the hour of your agony. Teach me to pray so that I can resist temptation and testify to you. Give me strength in my trials and boldness as your witness.

SUGGESTIONS FOR FACILITATORS, GROUP SESSION 5

1. Welcome group members and ask if anyone has any questions, announcements, or requests.

2. You may want to pray this prayer as a group:

God of Abraham, Isaac, and Jacob, you are the God of the living, and your authority extends to all people. May your will be done in our own lives and throughout the whole earth. Keep us focused on your promises, and instill in us the hope for your kingdom. As we reflect on the passion narratives of your beloved Son, guide us as we follow him faithfully. Help us to recognize our own weaknesses and our ability to betray him and deny our discipleship. Strengthen us with your word, and prepare us for life's most difficult hour.

3. Ask one or more of the following questions:
   - What most intrigued you from this week's study?
   - What makes you want to know and understand more of God's word?

4. Discuss lessons 19 through 24. Choose one or more of the questions for reflection and discussion from each lesson to talk over as a group.

5. Ask the group members to name one thing they have most appreciated about the way the group has worked during this Bible study. Ask group members to discuss any changes they might suggest in the way the group works in future studies.

6. Invite group members to complete lessons 25 through 30 on their own during the six days before the next meeting. They should write out their own answers to the questions as preparation for next week's session.

7. Ask group members what they find most fascinating about the ministry of Jesus in Luke's gospel. Discuss some of these insights in Luke's presentation of Jesus.

8. Conclude by praying aloud together the prayer at the end of one of the lessons discussed. You may want to conclude the prayer by asking members to voice prayers of thanksgiving.

"I have examined him in your presence and have not found this man guilty of any of your charges against him. Neither has Herod, for he sent him back to us." Luke 23:14-15

The Innocent Messiah Handed Over for Crucifixion

LUKE 23:1–25 ¹*Then the assembly rose as a body and brought Jesus before Pilate. ²They began to accuse him, saying, "We found this man perverting our nation, forbidding us to pay taxes to the emperor, and saying that he himself is the Messiah, a king." ³Then Pilate asked him, "Are you the king of the Jews?" He answered, "You say so." ⁴Then Pilate said to the chief priests and the crowds, "I find no basis for an accusation against this man." ⁵But they were insistent and said, "He stirs up the people by teaching throughout all Judea, from Galilee where he began even to this place."*

⁶*When Pilate heard this, he asked whether the man was a Galilean. ⁷And when he learned that he was under Herod's jurisdiction, he sent him off to Herod, who was himself in Jerusalem at that time. ⁸When Herod saw Jesus, he was very glad, for he had been wanting to see him for a long time, because he had heard about him and was hoping to see him perform some sign. ⁹He questioned him at some length, but Jesus gave him no answer. ¹⁰The chief priests and the scribes stood by, vehemently accusing him. ¹¹Even Herod with his soldiers*

*treated him with contempt and mocked him; then he put an elegant robe on him,
and sent him back to Pilate. ¹²That same day Herod and Pilate became friends
with each other; before this they had been enemies.*

*¹³Pilate then called together the chief priests, the leaders, and the people, ¹⁴and
said to them, "You brought me this man as one who was perverting the people;
and here I have examined him in your presence and have not found this man
guilty of any of your charges against him. ¹⁵Neither has Herod, for he sent him
back to us. Indeed, he has done nothing to deserve death. ¹⁶I will therefore have
him flogged and release him."*

*¹⁸Then they all shouted out together, "Away with this fellow! Release Barabbas
for us!" ¹⁹(This was a man who had been put in prison for an insurrection that
had taken place in the city, and for murder.) ²⁰Pilate, wanting to release Jesus,
addressed them again; ²¹but they kept shouting, "Crucify, crucify him!" ²²A third
time he said to them, "Why, what evil has he done? I have found in him no
ground for the sentence of death; I will therefore have him flogged and then
release him." ²³But they kept urgently demanding with loud shouts that he
should be crucified; and their voices prevailed. ²⁴So Pilate gave his verdict that
their demand should be granted. ²⁵He released the man they asked for, the one
who had been put in prison for insurrection and murder, and he handed Jesus
over as they wished.*

Since Roman authority was required to carry out the sentencing in
capital cases, the religious leaders bring Jesus before Pilate, the Roman
administrator of the region. In recounting the legal proceedings, Luke's
emphasis is on the innocence of Jesus and the widespread responsibility for
his death. Clearly his opponents try to paint Jesus as a revolutionary, accusing
him of threatening to undermine Roman authority. All of the charges against
Jesus are false: he taught non-violence, advocated paying taxes to Rome, and
never claimed political power. Pilate is convinced that Jesus is no threat and
declares him innocent (verse 4).

When the religious leaders insist that Jesus is stirring up people from
Galilee to Jerusalem, Pilate inquires whether Jesus is a Galilean. Finding him
to be under the jurisdiction of Herod, the tetrarch of Galilee, Pilate tries to
absolve himself of responsibility and sends Jesus to Herod, who was spending
the Passover in Jerusalem. Herod is thrilled at the prospect of seeing Jesus, for

he has wanted for a long time to watch him perform some sign. But Herod is disappointed when, after lengthy questioning, all he receives from Jesus is silence (verses 8–9). Even though the religious leaders continue accusing Jesus so that Herod might render a guilty verdict, Herod only ridicules him. He dresses Jesus in a regal robe to mock his royal claims and sends him back to Pilate. This cooperation between Pilate and Herod becomes an opportunity for amusement, and their formerly strained relationship becomes one of cooperation and friendship.

Again Pilate declares that he has not found Jesus guilty of the charges brought against him, and he confirms that Herod also has found him not guilty (verses 14–15). But although Jesus' innocence is legally proclaimed, he is retained in custody. Pilate tries three times to get Jesus released: first, offering to flog Jesus before he releases him (verse 16); second, seeking to substitute Barabbas for Jesus (verse 20); and third, insisting again that he finds no grounds for the sentence of death (verse 22). The leadership stirs up the crowd to insist that Jesus be crucified, and Pilate finally gives in to their demands.

The gospel narrative expresses the tragic injustice of Jesus' trial. The charges against Jesus are false, and Pilate spinelessly refuses to release the innocent Jesus. Pilate's primary concern was maintaining Roman order and control during the Passover festival. Given the choice between a controversial teacher and a riot in Jerusalem, Pilate decides that one death is better than mass violence. Neither the religious leaders nor the Roman governor are blameless in the death of Jesus. Both active and passive rejection of Jesus lead him to the cross and death.

Reflection and discussion

• What do I learn about Herod's character from this scene? Why did Jesus refuse to respond to him?

• Although Pilate and Herod found Jesus innocent, why did Pilate give in to the demands of those seeking the death of Jesus?

• Why is it so easy to capitulate in situations where we know we should stand our ground?

Prayer

Innocent Jesus, you were handed over to death by crucifixion to satisfy the crowds. Help me to realize that my refusal to stand up for justice and my sinful neglect to do what is right contribute to the tragedy of your death.

"We indeed have been condemned justly, for we are getting what we deserve for our deeds, but this man has done nothing wrong." Luke 23:41

Crucifixion Between Two Criminals

LUKE 23:26–43 *²⁶As they led him away, they seized a man, Simon of Cyrene, who was coming from the country, and they laid the cross on him, and made him carry it behind Jesus. ²⁷A great number of the people followed him, and among them were women who were beating their breasts and wailing for him. ²⁸But Jesus turned to them and said, "Daughters of Jerusalem, do not weep for me, but weep for yourselves and for your children. ²⁹For the days are surely coming when they will say, 'Blessed are the barren, and the wombs that never bore, and the breasts that never nursed.' ³⁰Then they will begin to say to the mountains, 'Fall on us'; and to the hills, 'Cover us.' ³¹For if they do this when the wood is green, what will happen when it is dry?"*

³²Two others also, who were criminals, were led away to be put to death with him. ³³When they came to the place that is called The Skull, they crucified Jesus there with the criminals, one on his right and one on his left. ³⁴Then Jesus said, "Father, forgive them; for they do not know what they are doing." And they cast lots to divide his clothing. ³⁵And the people stood by, watching; but the leaders scoffed at him, saying, "He saved others; let him save himself if he is the Messiah of God, his chosen one!" ³⁶The soldiers also mocked him, coming up and offering him sour wine, ³⁷and saying, "If you are the King of the Jews, save yourself!" ³⁸There was also an inscription over him, "This is the King of the Jews."

³⁹One of the criminals who were hanged there kept deriding him and saying, "Are you not the Messiah? Save yourself and us!" ⁴⁰But the other rebuked him, saying, "Do you not fear God, since you are under the same sentence of condemnation? ⁴¹And we indeed have been condemned justly, for we are getting what we deserve for our deeds, but this man has done nothing wrong." ⁴²Then he said, "Jesus, remember me when you come into your kingdom." ⁴³He replied, "Truly I tell you, today you will be with me in Paradise."

Jesus goes to his death carrying his own crossbeam, as was typical for Roman crucifixions. We can assume that Jesus was breaking down under the weight of the cross, so the executioners conscript Simon. Luke notes that Simon carried the cross "behind Jesus," providing a vivid image for what disciples must do. As Jesus had said, disciples must "take up their cross daily and follow me" (9:23; 14:27).

Freed from carrying the crossbeam, Jesus turns to gently address the women who were also following behind him and lamenting his crucifixion. They represent the people of Jerusalem and become the recipients of Jesus' final prophecy of the city's destruction. The women are mourning for Jesus, but Jesus tells them that they should be mourning for themselves and their children. Jesus wept over Jerusalem when he first entered it, and now as he exits its gates for the last time, he urges the women to weep for their city. Using several proverbs, Jesus describes the sufferings of Jerusalem's fall (verses 29-31). First, the usual blessedness of bearing children is reversed, and the barren are declared blessed. Second, people will desire a quick death, begging creation to collapse upon them. Third, Jesus compares his own suffering to green wood which is difficult to kindle and the suffering of Jerusalem to dry wood which is easy to kindle and to be consumed in fire. If Jesus who is innocent has experienced so much suffering, how much suffering awaits the guilty of Jerusalem.

Jesus' compassion is reflected throughout all the events surrounding his death. He even prays for his executioners, asking the Father to forgive them (verse 34). Ignorance is a poor defense in a court of law, but "they do not know what they are doing" is the best plea that Jesus can enter for them. Certainly this prayer is for the Roman soldiers carrying out the details of crucifixion, but it must also be for the religious leaders and all in the crowd whose pleas brought Jesus to the cross. Truly no one of them knew the significance of what they were doing.

Jesus is ridiculed by three different strata of society: the leaders, the soldiers, and a criminal. The group is inclusive, with Jewish rulers and Gentile soldiers joining in the mockery. The content of their derision is the same: though Jesus claims to be the Messiah, he cannot save himself. They scoff at both his identity and his mission.

The contrast between the two criminals on the right and left of Jesus is dramatic, representing the conflicting judgments that people will continue to make about Jesus. Luke alone recounts the exchange between the two criminals on their crosses and the dialogue between the repentant criminal and Jesus. The repentant one realizes who Jesus is, highlights his innocence in comparison with his own deeds, and asks for a share in Jesus' kingdom. Jesus looks for a reason to save sinners rather than for grounds to condemn, and this criminal provides him with sufficient reasons to save. He repents of his sins and has faith in Jesus, knowing that Jesus' death on the cross would lead to his coming into his kingdom. Emphasizing the saving effects of his own death for others, Jesus replies, "Truly I tell you, today you will be with me in Paradise" (verse 43). Despite what the mockery suggests, Jesus solemnly declares that he can and does save those who turn to him. Jesus' promise to him does not refer to some unspecified future, but to the immediate entry into paradise with Jesus. This garden-like state of happiness and peace is the heavenly realm where the righteous are gathered after death. This reconciled criminal is the final example and result of Jesus' mission to call sinners to repentance, to seek out and save the lost.

Reflection and discussion

• In what way does Jesus demonstrate his teachings on forgiveness during his passion? What challenge does his example offer to me?

• Jesus is mocked three times, each time with the challenge to save himself. What is the irony in these jeers? How does Jesus choose to save?

• How does the final exchange between Jesus and the criminal on the cross give me hope for myself and others?

• What is the most impressive thing about the character Jesus showed during his passion and death?

Prayer

Crucified Savior, help me trust that salvation is available through the weakness and self-surrender of the cross. Teach me how to take up the cross and follow after you each day.

Then Jesus, crying with a loud voice, said, "Father, into your hands I commend my spirit." Having said this, he breathed his last. Luke 23:46

The Death and Burial of Jesus

LUKE 23:44–56 ⁴⁴*It was now about noon, and darkness came over the whole land until three in the afternoon, ⁴⁵while the sun's light failed; and the curtain of the temple was torn in two. ⁴⁶Then Jesus, crying with a loud voice, said, "Father, into your hands I commend my spirit." Having said this, he breathed his last. ⁴⁷When the centurion saw what had taken place, he praised God and said, "Certainly this man was innocent." ⁴⁸And when all the crowds who had gathered there for this spectacle saw what had taken place, they returned home, beating their breasts. ⁴⁹But all his acquaintances, including the women who had followed him from Galilee, stood at a distance, watching these things.*

⁵⁰*Now there was a good and righteous man named Joseph, who, though a member of the council, ⁵¹had not agreed to their plan and action. He came from the Jewish town of Arimathea, and he was waiting expectantly for the kingdom of God. ⁵²This man went to Pilate and asked for the body of Jesus. ⁵³Then he took it down, wrapped it in a linen cloth, and laid it in a rock-hewn tomb where no one had ever been laid. ⁵⁴It was the day of Preparation, and the sabbath was beginning. ⁵⁵The women who had come with him from Galilee followed, and they saw the tomb and how his body was laid. ⁵⁶Then they returned, and prepared spices and ointments.*

On the sabbath they rested according to the commandment.

Jesus described his passion as the time for "the power of darkness," Satan's opportune time when darkness prevails. The heavens echo Jesus' description, as the sun's light is covered and darkness comes upon the earth as Jesus hangs on the cross. In this darkness the curtain of the temple, hiding the Holy of Holies, is torn in two. These signs express the cosmic and apocalyptic dimensions of Jesus' death as the focus of God's saving plan.

Because Luke has shown Jesus at prayer in all the critical moments of his life, Luke is the only gospel to narrate the death of Jesus with a prayer on his lips. This final prayer is from Psalm 31:5, and we can assume that Jesus prayed the entire psalm before he breathed his last. Throughout the passion, Jesus has been depicted as handed over into the hands of men, but now he entrusts himself into the hands of his Father. He places his life in God's hands and trusts that the Father will care for him. With this hope, Jesus expires.

At the end of the crucifixion scene, Luke gives emphasis to those who witness these events. The Gentile centurion, seeing the way that Jesus dies, praises God and declares the innocence of Jesus (verse 47). The crowds, presumably some of whom had demanded Jesus' crucifixion, went home beating their breasts, a sign of grief and contrition (verse 48). Luke is showing the saving quality of Jesus' death, as those who watched Jesus' final hours are moved to repentance. And finally, Jesus' acquaintances, including the women from Galilee, witness his death and remain faithful to the end.

Luke's passion account ends with the burial of Jesus by Joseph, a Jew from Arimathea. Although he was a member of the Sanhedrin, he had not agreed to their plan to put Jesus to death. In Acts, Luke will show that many Jewish leaders are sympathetic to the followers of Jesus and even join the faith. Joseph is described as "righteous" and "waiting expectantly for the kingdom of God," placing him in a long list of faithful Israelites, including Zechariah, Elizabeth, Simeon, and Anna, awaiting God's redemption. He is part of a faithful remnant, obedient in the midst of the unfaithfulness of others, participating in the fulfillment of God's promises to Israel.

Joseph requests the body of Jesus, cleanses his body for burial, wraps it in linen, and lays it in a tomb carved from rock in which no one had previously been buried. Although Jesus has died as a criminal, he is buried with honor.

Luke is careful to point out the obedience to the Sabbath law. Since it is nearing sundown and the Sabbath is about to begin, the women from Galilee take careful note of the tomb and Jesus' burial so that they could return after the Sabbath to anoint his body according to Jewish custom. When they returned home they prepared spices and perfumed oil in advance so that they could observe the proper Sabbath rest.

The burial scene forms a transition from the passion account to the resurrection. Both Joseph's burial of Jesus and the women's witness of the tomb establish that Jesus had indeed died and was buried in a unique tomb remembered by them all. The final note concerning the Sabbath rest forms a temporal bridge leading to the morning of resurrection.

Reflection and discussion

• Read Psalm 31 in its entirety. What insight does it offer to me in understanding the heart of Jesus during his final prayer to the Father?

• What have I learned from Luke's description of Jesus' crucifixion about the purpose and meaning of his death?

Prayer

I trust in you, O Lord. Let your face shine upon me, and save me in your steadfast love. You hear my prayer when I cry out to you for help. Into your hands I commend my spirit.

Now it was Mary Magdalene, Joanna, Mary the mother of James, and the other women with them who told this to the apostles. But these words seemed to them an idle tale, and they did not believe them. Luke 24:10–11

The Women Discover the Empty Tomb

LUKE 24:1–12 ¹*But on the first day of the week, at early dawn, they came to the tomb, taking the spices that they had prepared. ²They found the stone rolled away from the tomb, ³but when they went in, they did not find the body. ⁴While they were perplexed about this, suddenly two men in dazzling clothes stood beside them. ⁵The women were terrified and bowed their faces to the ground, but the men said to them, "Why do you look for the living among the dead? He is not here, but has risen. ⁶Remember how he told you, while he was still in Galilee, ⁷that the Son of Man must be handed over to sinners, and be crucified, and on the third day rise again." ⁸Then they remembered his words, ⁹and returning from the tomb, they told all this to the eleven and to all the rest. ¹⁰Now it was Mary Magdalene, Joanna, Mary the mother of James, and the other women with them who told this to the apostles. ¹¹But these words seemed to them an idle tale, and they did not believe them. ¹²But Peter got up and ran to the tomb; stooping and looking in, he saw the linen cloths by themselves; then he went home, amazed at what had happened.*

A ll of the gospels narrate the discovery of the empty tomb on the first day of the week, yet Luke recounts all of the events of his final chapter as happening on this same day. This is the first day of a new age, the day Christians will set apart each week as the day of resurrection. Luke's unique way of describing the discovery of the empty tomb and the resurrection appearances brings his plan for the gospel to its finale and forms a transition to his second volume, the Acts of the Apostles.

On arriving at the tomb, the women find the stone rolled away, but they do not find the body of Jesus. Although, to the reader of the gospel, the empty tomb might hint at a reversal of the tragedy of Jesus' death, it only left the women perplexed. Then the sight of two heavenly messengers terrifies the women, and they bow to the ground. The angels challenge the women's focus on the tomb: "Why do you look for the living among the dead?" (verse 5). This is similar to the challenge given by the two men in white garments at the ascension of Jesus: "Why do you stand looking up toward heaven?" (Acts 1:11). After each challenging question, the angels proclaim the message that sets the hearers off on their mission.

Jesus has risen from the dead, just as he told his disciples he would. Yet, when Jesus foretold his resurrection during his ministry, the disciples must have thought he was referring to resurrection at the end of time. But now the message of Christ's resurrection is proclaimed before his empty tomb. Although it seems too unbelievable to be true, the women return and tell their experience to the apostles. For the first time, the apostles hear of the empty tomb, the angelic presence, and the announcement that Jesus has risen just as he said he would.

The women's story seems like an absurd attempt to challenge reality. No one believes them, except perhaps Peter. His denials have instilled in him a greater trust. He runs to the tomb, peers into the tomb, and sees only the linen cloths without the body of Jesus, just as the women have said. The cloths suggest that Jesus has previously been in the tomb, but is no longer. If the body of Jesus has been stolen, surely the cloths would not still be there. Peter is left in amazement.

Luke invites his readers, along with the disciples, to ponder this mystery. Perplexity, disbelief, and amazement mix with hints of something more wondrous than anyone can imagine. What can explain these events? Could Jesus be alive after all? Do we dare to hope in the resurrection? What seems to have been an end has now become a new beginning.

Reflection and discussion

• How does Luke's gospel present the events at the empty tomb as a moment of reflection, decision, and faith for his readers?

• What might Peter be pondering as he heard the message from the women and ran to the tomb?

• How do I proclaim the message of resurrection to friends, family, and associates?

Prayer

God of the living, help me to trust in the good news of your Son's resurrection and allow that message to transform my life. Increase my faith in Christ's victory and my awareness of his presence in my life.

"Were not our hearts burning within us while
he was talking to us on the road, while he was
opening the scriptures to us?" Luke 24:32

Burning Hearts and Broken Bread

LUKE 24:13–35 ¹³*Now on that same day two of them were going to a village called Emmaus, about seven miles from Jerusalem,* ¹⁴*and talking with each other about all these things that had happened.* ¹⁵*While they were talking and discussing, Jesus himself came near and went with them,* ¹⁶*but their eyes were kept from recognizing him.* ¹⁷*And he said to them, "What are you discussing with each other while you walk along?" They stood still, looking sad.* ¹⁸*Then one of them, whose name was Cleopas, answered him, "Are you the only stranger in Jerusalem who does not know the things that have taken place there in these days?"* ¹⁹*He asked them, "What things?" They replied, "The things about Jesus of Nazareth, who was a prophet mighty in deed and word before God and all the people,* ²⁰*and how our chief priests and leaders handed him over to be condemned to death and crucified him.* ²¹*But we had hoped that he was the one to redeem Israel. Yes, and besides all this, it is now the third day since these things took place.* ²²*Moreover, some women of our group astounded us. They were at*

*the tomb early this morning, ²³and when they did not find his body there, they
came back and told us that they had indeed seen a vision of angels who said that
he was alive. ²⁴Some of those who were with us went to the tomb and found it
just as the women had said; but they did not see him." ²⁵Then he said to them,
"Oh, how foolish you are, and how slow of heart to believe all that the prophets
have declared! ²⁶Was it not necessary that the Messiah should suffer these things
and then enter into his glory?" ²⁷Then beginning with Moses and all the prophets, he interpreted to them the things about himself in all the scriptures.*

*²⁸As they came near the village to which they were going, he walked ahead as
if he were going on. ²⁹But they urged him strongly, saying, "Stay with us, because
it is almost evening and the day is now nearly over." So he went in to stay with
them. ³⁰When he was at the table with them, he took bread, blessed and broke
it, and gave it to them. ³¹Then their eyes were opened, and they recognized him;
and he vanished from their sight. ³²They said to each other, "Were not our hearts
burning within us while he was talking to us on the road, while he was opening
the scriptures to us?" ³³That same hour they got up and returned to Jerusalem;
and they found the eleven and their companions gathered together. ³⁴They were
saying, "The Lord has risen indeed, and he has appeared to Simon!" ³⁵Then they
told what had happened on the road, and how he had been made known to
them in the breaking of the bread.*

Cleopas and his unnamed companion have been disciples of Jesus, but
their hopes have been dashed by the events during the Passover feast
in Jerusalem. Now they are returning home to the village of Emmaus
to resume their daily lives. Even though they have heard reports that the tomb
of Jesus is empty and the angels' message that he is alive, they walked along
sad and disappointed, shorn of hope.

As they travel on their way, they discuss everything that has happened—
Jesus' torturous death, their disappointed hopes, and the women's report of
the empty tomb. When Jesus comes up to them, he seems to be another pil-
grim returning home. The question of Cleopas, "Are you the only stranger in
Jerusalem who does not know the things that have taken place there in these
days?" (verse 18), assumes that the crucifixion of Jesus was the talk of
Jerusalem during the Passover feast. Ironically, it is Cleopas and his companion who really don't know what has taken place. They express their sadness at

the death of Jesus, their disappointment and shattered hopes, and their skepticism at the women's report.

The response of Jesus is surprisingly forceful, reproaching them for not taking the Scriptures seriously regarding the suffering and glorification of the Messiah (verses 25–26). Jesus' interpretation of the Scriptures to them does not seem to refer to any particular passage. Rather, he lays out for them the way in which "all the Scriptures" have led up to God's revelation of the cross and resurrection of Christ (verse 27). He shows that the ancient Scriptures, "beginning with Moses and all the prophets," prepare for the gospel and are fulfilled in Jesus.

The two disciples offer hospitality and convince Jesus to stay with them. When at table with them, Jesus "took bread, blessed and broke it, and gave it to them" (verse 30). His liturgical gestures look back to the action of the Last Supper and forward to the "breaking of the bread" in Acts. As the narrative reaches its climax and Jesus vanishes from their sight, the disciples realize that they were experiencing the presence of the risen Christ all along. They remembered that their hearts were catching fire with insight and love as Jesus interpreted the Scriptures for them (verse 32). Only after understanding the Scriptures were they prepared to recognize Jesus in the breaking of the bread.

Through the Emmaus account, the disciples and Luke's readers realize how the risen Lord will be present to his church. The encounter demonstrates the dynamic relationship between word and sacrament in the life of the church, and it reflects the twofold structure of Christian assembly. Both the interpretation of the Scriptures and the breaking of the bread are actions of the risen Christ in which his presence is made real for the church.

But the account suggests the Christian Eucharist not only in word and sacrament, but also in the movement from table to witness. The disciples return at once to Jerusalem to communicate their experience of how they came to know the risen Christ (verses 33-35). The narrative begins with the disciples walking slowly and hopelessly from Jerusalem to Emmaus, and it ends with their movement hurriedly and expectantly from Emmaus to Jerusalem with the good news of the risen Lord.

Reflection and discussion

• What is the significance in the fact that Luke places all his resurrection narratives on the same day, the first day of the week?

• In what ways does coming to know and understand the Torah and prophets of Israel open my eyes to know and recognize Jesus?

• What does the Emmaus account teach me about the ways that Jesus reveals himself to me today?

Prayer

Risen Lord, open the Scriptures to me so that you may also open my eyes, mind, and heart to you. Assure me of your presence with me when I study the Bible, so that my heart will burn with understanding and love.

"These are my words that I spoke to you while I was still with you—
that everything written about me in the law of Moses, the prophets,
and the psalms must be fulfilled." Then he opened their minds
to understand the scriptures. Luke 24:44-45

Commission to All Nations
and Promise of the Spirit

LUKE 24:36-53 ³⁶*While they were talking about this, Jesus himself stood among them and said to them, "Peace be with you." ³⁷They were startled and terrified, and thought that they were seeing a ghost. ³⁸He said to them, "Why are you frightened, and why do doubts arise in your hearts? ³⁹Look at my hands and my feet; see that it is I myself. Touch me and see; for a ghost does not have flesh and bones as you see that I have." ⁴⁰And when he had said this, he showed them his hands and his feet. ⁴¹While in their joy they were disbelieving and still wondering, he said to them, "Have you anything here to eat?" ⁴²They gave him a piece of broiled fish, ⁴³and he took it and ate in their presence.*

⁴⁴*Then he said to them, "These are my words that I spoke to you while I was still with you—that everything written about me in the law of Moses, the prophets, and the psalms must be fulfilled." ⁴⁵Then he opened their minds to understand the scriptures, ⁴⁶and he said to them, "Thus it is written, that the Messiah is to suffer and to rise from the dead on the third day, ⁴⁷and that repentance and forgiveness of sins is to be proclaimed in his name to all nations, beginning from*

Jerusalem. 48You are witnesses of these things. 49And see, I am sending upon you what my Father promised; so stay here in the city until you have been clothed with power from on high."

50Then he led them out as far as Bethany, and, lifting up his hands, he blessed them. 51While he was blessing them, he withdrew from them and was carried up into heaven. 52And they worshiped him, and returned to Jerusalem with great joy; 53and they were continually in the temple blessing God.

The close of Luke's gospel confirms the reality of Jesus' resurrection and commissions the disciples for their universal mission. The account elicits a number of emotional responses from the disciples. At first, they are startled, terrified, frightened, and incredulous (verses 37-38). Yet, Jesus stands in their midst and says, "Peace be with you." His greeting wishes for them a fullness and wholeness that is brought about by Christ's victory over all sources of fear. After Jesus demonstrates that he is real, their fear turns to joy, though they are still disbelieving (verse 41). But now their unbelief seems to have more to do with the feeling that it is all too good to be true. By the end of the account, the disciples worship Jesus, they are filled with great joy, and they continually give thanks and praise to God in the temple.

The first emphasis in this resurrection account is the real and bodily presence of Jesus. The risen reality of Jesus is impossible to completely describe or understand, because it belongs to the age to come, rather than to the limitations of the present era. At first the disciples suppose they are seeing some kind of insubstantial, ghostly presence. But Jesus emphasizes his "flesh and bones" (verse 39), suggesting that he shares a common humanity with them. He invites them to take a look at his hands and feet, to touch him in order to know that his body is real. The narrative counters arguments that the disciples perhaps saw nothing more than a fleeting vision or a grief-induced hallucination. Jesus is indeed real and recognizable. He even eats a piece of broiled fish in their presence as a final proof, since ghosts and visions do not eat (verses 42-43). "See that it is I myself," Jesus insists. Surely this is the same Jesus who lived among them before his death. The risen Lord is the man of Galilee.

The second emphasis in this narrative is the necessity of Jesus' suffering and resurrection in God's plan. Jesus is the heart of the ancient Scriptures. He is the fulfillment of everything written about him "in the law of Moses, the prophets, and the psalms" (verse 44). Jesus opens the disciples' minds by opening the Scriptures to them. In light of the resurrection, the disciples are now able to understand how the whole of the Old Testament teachings fit together as promise and are completed in the dying and rising of Jesus the Messiah.

Jesus summarizes God's fundamental plan as revealed in Scripture with three infinitives: to suffer, to rise, and to proclaim (verses 46-47). The Scriptures teach that the Messiah would suffer and rise from the dead, and that a message of repentance and forgiveness would be proclaimed to all nations as a result. The first two of these elements of God's plan have just been completed, and the last remains for the disciples to carry out. Jesus then commissions his disciples for the decisive role they are to play in the new and final phase of salvation history: they are to be witnesses to Jesus Christ, proclaiming repentance and forgiveness, beginning in Jerusalem and extending to the whole world. It is this witness of the disciples that is the subject of Luke's second volume, the Acts of the Apostles. The goal of Jesus' journey to Jerusalem now becomes the starting point from which the message of salvation will extend to the ends of the earth (Acts 1:8).

The gospel concludes with Jesus' promise to send the Holy Spirit and the ascension of Jesus to the Father. Although his resurrection appearances have come to an end, the church will continue to experience his glorified presence and activity in many ways. As the gospel closes, the disciples are left waiting in Jerusalem for what God will do next. Luke's sequel volume will continue the story of the church, beginning with the descent of the Holy Spirit and the empowerment of the disciples as witnesses to all the nations.

Reflection and discussion

• In what ways is the church a witness to Jesus Christ in the world today? How is my life a part of that witness?

• Why is it so important for Christians to know "the law of Moses, the prophets, and the psalms" in order to give witness to Jesus?

• In what sense is Luke's gospel incomplete? What is necessary to complete it?

• What is the most important message or insight I take away from the Gospel according to Luke?

Prayer

Risen Lord, send your Holy Spirit upon me so that I may be filled with joy and empowered to be your witness. Help me to recognize you as you make your presence known in word, sacrament, and the lives of your disciples today.

SUGGESTIONS FOR FACILITATORS, GROUP SESSION 6

1. Welcome group members and make any final announcements or requests.

2. You may want to pray this prayer as a group:

Father of our Lord Jesus Christ, you have given us the inspired words of the Gospel according to Luke so that we may come to know Jesus as the Savior of all people and Lord of all nations. He is the fulfillment of your saving plan made known in the Torah, the prophets, and the psalms. Through his death on the cross and his glorious resurrection, Jesus has commissioned us to proclaim repentance and forgiveness to all. May the good news of your Son's resurrection deepen our trust in his victory over sin and death and transform our lives through your Holy Spirit.

3. Ask one or more of the following questions:
   - How has this study of Luke's gospel enriched your life?
   - In what way has this study challenged you the most?

4. Discuss lessons 25 through 30. Choose one or more of the questions for reflection and discussion from each lesson to discuss as a group.

5. Ask the group if they would like to study another in the Threshold Bible Study series. Discuss the topic and dates, and make a decision among those interested. Ask the group members to suggest people they would like to invite to participate in the next study series.

6. Ask the group to discuss the insights that stand out most from this study over the past six weeks.

7. Conclude by praying aloud the following prayer or another of your own choosing:

Holy Spirit of the living God, you inspired the writers of the Scriptures and you have guided our study during these weeks. Continue to deepen our love for the word of God in the holy Scriptures, and draw us more deeply into the heart of Jesus. We thank you for the confident hope you have placed within us and the gifts that build up the church. Through this study, lead us to worship and witness more fully and fervently, and bless us now and always with the fire of your love.

The GOSPEL OF LUKE
in the Sunday Lectionary

LUKE 1:1-4; 4:14-21
3rd Sunday in Ordinary Time
(69C)

LUKE 1:26-38
4th Sunday of Advent
(11-B)

LUKE 1:39-45
4th Sunday of Advent
(12-C)

LUKE 1:46-48, 49-50, 53-54
3rd Sunday of Advent (resp.)
(8-B)

LUKE 2:1-14
Christmas: Mass at Midnight
(14-ABC)

LUKE 2:15-20
Christmas: Mass at Dawn
(15-ABC)

LUKE 2:22-40 OR 2:22, 39-40
Sunday in Octave of Christmas: Holy Family
(17-B)

LUKE 2:41-52
Sunday in Octave of Christmas: Holy Family
(17-C)

LUKE 3:1-6
2nd Sunday of Advent
(6-C)

LUKE 3:10-18
3rd Sunday of Advent
(9-C)

THE GOSPEL OF LUKE IN THE SUNDAY LECTIONARY

LUKE 3:15-16, 21-22
Sunday after Epiphany:
Baptism of the Lord *(21-C)*

LUKE 4:1-13
1st Sunday of Lent
(24-C)

LUKE 4:14-21 (WITH 1:1-4)
3rd Sunday in Ordinary Time
(69-C)

LUKE 4:21-30
4th Sunday in Ordinary Time
(72-C)

LUKE 5:1-11
5th Sunday in Ordinary Time
(75-C)

LUKE 6:17, 20-26
6th Sunday in Ordinary Time
(78-C)

LUKE 6:27-38
7th Sunday in Ordinary Time
(81-C)

LUKE 6:39-45
8th Sunday in Ordinary Time
(84-C)

LUKE 7:1-10
9th Sunday in Ordinary Time
(87-C)

LUKE 7:11-17
10th Sunday in Ordinary Time
(90-C)

LUKE 7:36—8:3 OR 7:36-50
11th Sunday in Ordinary Time
(93-C)

LUKE 9:11B-17
Sunday after Trinity Sun:
Body & Blood of Christ *(169-C)*

LUKE 9:18-24
12th Sunday in Ordinary Time
(96-C)

LUKE 9:28B-36
2nd Sunday of Lent
(27-C)

LUKE 9:51-62
13th Sunday in Ordinary Time
(99-C)

LUKE 10:1-12, 17-20 OR 10:1-9
14th Sunday in Ordinary Time
(102-C)

THE GOSPEL OF LUKE IN THE SUNDAY LECTIONARY

LUKE 17:5-10
27th Sunday in Ordinary Time
(141-C)

LUKE 17:11-19
28th Sunday in Ordinary Time
(144-C)

LUKE 18:1-8
29th Sunday in Ordinary Time
(147-C)

LUKE 18:9-14
30th Sunday in Ordinary Time
(150-C)

LUKE 19:1-10
31st Sunday in Ordinary Time
(153-C)

LUKE 19:28-40
Palm Sunday: Procession of Palms
(37-C)

LUKE 20:27-38 OR 20:27, 34-38
32nd Sunday in Ordinary Time
(156-C)

LUKE 21:5-19
33rd Sunday in Ordinary Time
(159-C)

LUKE 21:25-28, 34-36
1st Sunday of Advent
(3-C)

LUKE 22:14—23:56 OR 23:1-49
Palm Sunday Mass
(38-C)

LUKE 23:35-43
34th Sunday in Ordinary Time:
Christ the King *(162-C)*

LUKE 24:1-12
Easter Vigil
(41-C)

LUKE 24:13-35
Easter Sunday: Resurrection of the Lord
(opt. 2) *(42-ABC)*

LUKE 24:13-35
3rd Sunday of Easter
(46-A)

LUKE 24:35-48
3rd Sunday of Easter
(47-B)

LUKE 24:46-53
Ascension of the Lord
(58-C)

Ordering Additional Studies

AVAILABLE TITLES IN THIS SERIES INCLUDE...

Advent Light

Angels of God

Divine Mercy

Eucharist

The Feasts of Judaism

Forgiveness

God's Spousal Love

The Holy Spirit and Spiritual Gifts

Jerusalem, the Holy City

Missionary Discipleship

Mysteries of the Rosary

The Names of Jesus

Peacemaking and Nonviolence

People of the Passion

Pilgrimage in the Footsteps of Jesus

The Resurrection and the Life

The Sacred Heart of Jesus

Stewardship of the Earth

The Tragic and Triumphant Cross

Jesus, the Messianic King
PART 1: Matthew 1–16
PART 2: Matthew 17–28

Jesus, the Suffering Servant
PART 1: Mark 1–8
PART 2: Mark 9–16

Jesus, the Compassionate Savior
PART 1: Luke 1–11
PART 2: Luke 12–24

Jesus, the Word Made Flesh
PART 1: John 1–10
PART 2: John 11–21

Church of the Holy Spirit
PART 1: Acts of the Apostles 1–14
PART 2: Acts of the Apostles 15–28

Salvation Offered for All People:
Romans

Proclaiming Christ Crucified:
1 Corinthians

The Lamb and the Beasts:
The Book of Revelation

TO CHECK AVAILABILITY OR FOR A DESCRIPTION
OF EACH STUDY, VISIT OUR WEBSITE AT
www.ThresholdBibleStudy.com
OR CALL US AT **1-800-321-0411**

TWENTY-THIRD
PUBLICATIONS